Behind Enemy Lines

Behind Enemy Lines

Brother Andrew

Based on the life of
Andrew van der Bijl

Nancy Drummond

CF4·K

10 9 8 7 6 5 4 3 2 1
© Copyright 2014 Nancy Drummond
Paperback ISBN: 978-1-78191-297-3
epub ISBN: 978-1-78191-338-3
mobi ISBN: 978-1-78191-339-0

Published by
Christian Focus Publications,
Geanies House, Fearn, Tain, Ross-shire,
IV20 1TW, Scotland, U.K.
Tel: 01862 871011
Fax: 01862 871699
www.christianfocus.com
email: info@christianfocus.com

Cover design by Daniel van Straaten
Cover illustration by Jeff Anderson
American English is used throughout this book
Printed and bound in Denmark by Nørhaven

Scripture quotations are taken from
the King James Version of the Bible.

All rights reserved. No part of this publication may be reproduced, stored in a retrieval system, or transmitted, in any form, by any means, electronic, mechanical, photocopying, recording or otherwise without the prior permission of the publisher or a licence permitting restricted copying. In the U.K. such licences are issued by the Copyright Licensing Agency, Saffron House, 6-10 Kirby Street, London, EC1 8TS. www.cla.co.uk

This book is written in a conversational style. Its use of dialogue is fictional, but used in such a way as to get across facts and history with a relaxed and easily read approach.

Contents

On a Mission of Mischief

It was a perfect opportunity—too good to pass up. In the little kitchen, Mrs Whetstra slid a batch of cookies into the wood-burning stove as she joyfully hummed a hymn. Just outside the kitchen, a large pane of new window glass leaned against the front of the house. Andrew van der Bijl's slender, young frame shook with excitement. This was his chance to prove the Whetstras were not such good Christians after all.

Andrew quickly removed his clunky wooden shoes and crept from his hiding place beneath an old fishmonger's cart. He carefully shouldered the wide pane of glass and dashed to the ladder that led to the Whetstras' thatched roof. With an evil grin, Andrew nimbly climbed the ladder and centered the glass on top of the chimney, completely blocking it. Then he flew down the ladder and back to the safety of the dilapidated cart.

Within minutes, the prank was accomplishing its purpose. Andrew watched Mrs Whetstra come back into the kitchen, which had filled with thick smoke.

She immediately began to cough, waving her apron in a feeble attempt to clear the air.

"Phillip!" she choked out. "Phillip, come quickly!"

Mrs Whetstra threw open the oven door just as Mr Whetstra ran into the room. The little stove belched smoke.

"Get outside," Mr Whetstra ordered, gently ushering his wife toward the door. "I'm going to the roof."

Andrew was disappointed by the lack of profanity and angry outbursts. Still, he had to smother a giggle at the look on Mr Whetstra's face when he spotted the glass on the chimney. Mr Whetstra snatched up the pane of glass and looked around the yard. Andrew shrank deeper into his hiding place. Mr Whetstra climbed slowly down the ladder and leaned the glass against the house. He glared around the yard one more time, his eyes lingering dangerously on the fishmonger's cart. Andrew held his breath. Finally, Mr Whetstra sighed, shook his head, and led his wife back inside. Andrew grinned. Success!

Andrew was well-known around his little town of Witte, Holland as a prankster and a troublemaker. He wasn't truly bad, and he never tried to hurt anyone, but he longed for excitement and intrigue that was foreign to his sleepy little village. More than anything, Andrew wanted to be a spy, a smuggler, a saboteur, or a superhero. He was forever sneaking around, creating secret campaigns and embarking on missions of mischief.

Sometimes Andrew's exploits were harmless, but other times they had costly consequences. With a shortage of real enemies, the boys of Witte often fought one another, battling fiercely with their wooden shoes, called klompen. One afternoon, in a desperate showdown, Andrew broke his klompen on the head of his best friend, Kees. In the aftermath of the fight, Kees and Andrew stared down at the broken shoe.

"What will your father say?" Kees wondered quietly.

Andrew swallowed hard. Papa already got up before dawn to weed the garden and then rode his bicycle four miles to his blacksmithing job in another town. After working hard all day, he rode the four miles back home, often after dark. Money was tight and time was even tighter. There was no money for new klompen and no time to repair broken ones. Papa would not be happy.

"He won't say anything compared with what your mama will say when she sees that bump on your head!" Andrew teased, trying to make his voice light.

Kees reached up and gingerly touched the rapidly swelling knot on his forehead. He winced. Then both boys looked at each other and burst out laughing.

"It was a good fight," Kees admitted.

"One for the record books," Andrew agreed, linking arms with his best friend. "And there is no one whose head I would rather break my shoe on!"

But as the boys parted and Andrew headed toward home, his sense of dread began to grow. He hated to disappoint Papa. With a heavy heart and a shoeless foot, Andrew faced Papa. He held up the broken klompen.

"I broke my shoe, Papa," Andrew admitted quietly.

Papa, nearly deaf from years of work in a noisy blacksmith shop, shook his head and furrowed his brow. "Speak up," he urged in his too-loud voice.

Andrew took a deep breath. "I broke my shoe, Papa," he nearly shouted.

"Oh, Andrew," Papa boomed. "You must learn to be more careful."

Papa took the klompen and worked late into the night beside the old oil lamp, carefully repairing the wooden shoe. As Andrew watched his father work, he felt a twinge of regret. He knew he caused Papa headaches and heartaches with his escapades, but the drive for adventure was just too strong. Soon, Andrew found himself in the middle of another quest.

Andrew's older brother Ben worked hard after school and on weekends, doing odd jobs to earn pennies. In Andrew's mind, Ben was an enemy, a wealthy secret agent for some foreign government. One afternoon, Andrew's vivid imagination got the best of him, and he snuck up to Ben's attic hideaway while Ben was in the village on a job. Andrew was determined to take his arch enemy down.

Avoiding imaginary guards at every turn, Andrew found Ben's prized possession: an old piggy bank filled with pennies he had earned. Carefully sliding a pocketknife into the opening, Andrew shook twenty-five pennies onto the floor. He stuffed his pockets full and carefully replaced the piggy bank. Then he slipped from the attic into the yard to enjoy his treasures.

As he fingered the coins, Andrew realized he had a problem. Twenty-five pennies was a great deal of money for a young boy in those days. If he walked into the candy shop to spend it—as he had dreamed of doing— the shopkeeper would certainly ask Andrew where he got so much money. But his spoils were worthless if he couldn't enjoy them. Then Andrew had a brilliant idea.

"Miss Meekle?" Andrew said timidly as he approached his teacher the next day at school. "Look what I found."

Andrew held up his cupped hands, filled with all twenty-five pennies. Miss Meekle's eyes widened.

"Can I keep it?" Andrew asked.

"Well, Andy, that's a lot of money," Miss Meekle said, rubbing her chin thoughtfully. "Are you sure you don't know who it belongs to?"

Andrew gulped. "No, Miss Meekle," he lied. "I found it on the road outside our school."

Miss Meekle thought for a moment. Then her face brightened. "Of course, Andy! You must take it to the police. They will know what to do with it."

Andrew's heart constricted. The police? They would see him as the criminal he was for sure! But now that he had told Miss Meekle about the money, there was no way out. With leaden feet, Andrew slunk toward the little town hall where the police chief's office was. His insides quivered.

The police chief listened to Andrew's story. "Tell me again where you found the money," he prompted.

Andrew repeated his lie. "I found it in the street."

"And you have no idea whose it is?" the chief asked.

"No, sir," Andrew lied again.

The police chief peered at Andrew over his spectacles for a moment, studying him carefully. Then he opened a drawer in his heavy desk. Andrew closed his eyes, sure he was about to be handcuffed.

"Here, Andrew," the chief said.

Andrew opened his eyes. The police chief was holding out an envelope. Andrew took it hesitantly.

"Put the money in the envelope," the chief instructed. "We'll write your name on the outside. In one year, if no one has claimed it, the money will be yours."

A whole year? That was an eternity! Andrew reluctantly put the money in the envelope and handed it to the police chief. One year later, Andrew made his trip to the candy shop. Ben had not mentioned the missing pennies, and of course no one else had claimed the money. As he sucked on his candy, Andrew silently congratulated himself on his skills. He had successfully completed another adventure without being captured.

Andrew was an expert at evading capture on his missions of mischief, but he also became skilled at avoiding capture in his escapes from church. Sundays were a day of worship in the van der Bijl household, and every Sunday morning the family would walk together to the Protestant church on the far end of Witte. Because it was so hard for Papa to hear, they always sat together in the front row, filing solemnly into a pew that was not quite long enough to hold the entire family.

Andrew soon learned that if he deliberately walked slower than the rest of the family on the walk to church, he would be last into the pew, and he would be the person who didn't quite fit. So, Andrew always stayed a few steps behind his siblings. Then, when the pew was full, he would generously offer to find himself a seat further back in the congregation. With Mama and Papa's blessing, Andrew would move further and further back in the building until he had slipped right out the door.

In the summer, Andrew spent his Sundays basking on the sunny polders—wide fields that surrounded Witte. In the winter, he used his wooden klompen to happily skate along the frozen canals that crisscrossed the town. Because nearly everyone in Witte attended church, there was no one to challenge Andrew as to why he wasn't in the service.

Andrew always seemed to know when the service was winding down. As the church service came to an end, he would slip back into the building and station himself near the preacher as the worshippers emerged from the doors. Although he looked like he was waiting patiently for his parents, Andrew was really gathering "intel," making mental notes of the comments the congregation made about the sermon. By the time Mama and Papa finally emerged from their front-row position, Andrew usually knew the text and theme of the sermon, as well as the key points and illustrations.

On Sunday afternoons in Holland, the men gathered in living rooms around the villages to drink strong black coffee and discuss current events and—most importantly—the Sunday sermon. With a pounding heart and clammy hands, Andrew would join Papa in these discussions, throwing out thoughts and ideas gleaned from the townspeople as they exited the service. Andrew's careful comments convinced everyone that he not only attended church, but was actively engaged in the services. No one ever suspected he had sat through only a handful of them.

Andrew grew increasingly comfortable living a life of deception and lies. After a while, his stories seemed more real than the truths of his life. But the foundations of Andrew's reality were about to be shaken, and his quiet, carefree life would never be the same.

At Work and at War in Witte

Life in the van der Bijl household was always filled with chores and challenges. Andrew grew up peeling potatoes, shining shoes, and helping Ben push the paddles on the washing machine, a heavy wooden contraption that was Mama's pride and joy. There was always something to do, some task to accomplish. And because money was often tight, everything was about doing more with less and wasting nothing.

Only one family member was exempt from the work. Andrew's oldest brother, Bas, was six years older than he was, but Bas had the heart and mind of a small child. He spent his days beneath an old elm tree, watching the world go by and waving enthusiastically at the villagers who passed. Every evening, Andrew or one of his siblings would gently lead Bas home for dinner. But although Bas never learned to speak or dress himself, he was a musical prodigy. In the evenings, after the family supper, Bas would make the old pump organ sing like no one else could. The townspeople of Witte would cluster outside the little house in the gathering shadows to enjoy the sweet melodies of Bas's special gift.

When Bas became ill in 1939, Andrew was heartbroken. The doctor said it was tuberculosis—very deadly and highly contagious—and there was nothing he could do. Mama and Papa set up sleeping quarters in the living room and gave their little room to Bas. Andrew mournfully listened to Bas coughing and peeked into the room frequently, watching the already slender frame become skeletal. In his heart, Andrew knew Bas would be leaving them soon, but he couldn't bear the thought of letting go of his dear brother.

To prevent the spread of the tuberculosis, only Mama and the doctor were allowed into the room where Bas slept fitfully. But a few days after his eleventh birthday, in May 1939, Andrew had a plan. While Mama was busy in the kitchen, Andrew crept into the room and flung himself across the bed, right on top of Bas.

"God," Andrew sobbed, praying aloud, "I've never really asked you for anything. So please give me this one thing. Don't take my Bas away from me. And if you are going to take Bas away, please take me too. I can't go on without him."

Then Andrew kissed Bas again and again on the mouth, desperately trying to catch his illness. But in July, Bas died, and Andrew did not. In fact he was as fit as a fiddle - not even a sniffle. Andrew was angry. He felt like God had failed him.

There was little time for Andrew to enjoy his self-pity. Just two months after Bas died, in September 1939, the government of Holland called for a mobilization against the growing Nazi regime in nearby Germany. Army reserves were activated and all private vehicles were turned over to the government. Cars lumbered down the once-quiet streets of Witte on their way to government surrendering stations. There was nothing normal about life anymore.

Some days, Andrew lingered under the old elm where Bas used to stand. Other days, he found himself at the Whetstras'. His old enemies seemed like a calming presence in Witte's dark days, and Andrew found himself craving their quiet, confident kindness in the wake of the chaos that had overtaken his world.

"Hello, Andrew," Mrs Whetstra would greet him warmly whenever he sauntered past their windows.

"Hello, Mrs Whetstra," he would answer, slowing his steps.

Sometimes she would ask where he was going. Sometimes she would ask about his mother. Sometimes she would share a piece of news she had heard. But she always had a ready smile and a plate full of cookies.

"Thank you, ma'am," Andrew would say, taking a cookie from the plate.

"You're a good boy, Andrew," Mrs Whetstra would say with another smile, patting his head.

"Yes, ma'am," Andrew would answer, but he always felt a twinge of guilt when he remembered the pane of glass over the chimney so long ago. He wondered if the Whetstras would ever know it had been him.

One afternoon Mr Whetstra was home, and he came to the window to stand beside his wife. His kind eyes seemed to see straight into Andrew's soul. Andrew instinctively hid his cookie behind his back.

"Have you seen anything new in your travels today, Andrew?" he asked.

"No, sir," Andrew answered, shifting his weight nervously from foot to foot.

"They are coming, Andrew," Mr Whetstra speculated, looking away toward some unseen horizon. "Soon they will be here with their heavy steps and hateful hearts."

"Yes, sir."

"Andrew, are you praying for your country?" Mr Whetstra asked, turning his eyes back to the boy in front of him.

"Yes, sir."

"Good," Mr Whetstra said with a sigh. "We will need all the prayers we can get." He reached out to ruffle Andrew's hair. "Now, run along and be good."

Andrew turned quickly, still carrying his precious, uneaten cookie. As he reached the edge of the yard, Andrew heard Mr Whetstra call out from the window.

"You can eat your cookie, Andrew," he said. "Our old stove hasn't smoked at all since I put in my new window."

Andrew spun around. Mr Whetstra winked, and then chuckled at the surprised look on Andrew's face. Then he shook his head and ducked back inside.

Andrew was stunned. Mr Whetstra had known about the prank all along. 'Why hadn't he told Papa?' Andrew wondered. Why did Mr Whetstra want him to pray for Holland? Clearly, God was not interested in the prayers of a wayward little boy. Bas dying was proof of that in Andrew's mind. Besides, Andrew wasn't sure even prayers could stop the German invasion. Mr Whetstra himself had said they would arrive soon. And when they did come, Andrew planned to counter-attack with something much stronger than prayer.

By April 1940, the government of Holland was purposely flooding the fields in a feeble attempt to delay the inevitable German advance. As water flooded the polders, refugees flooded Witte, simultaneously escaping the water and the Nazis. They filled the houses of Witte, squeezing into already-crowded homes, making the village seem overstuffed and explosive. Everyone tried to go about their daily business, but there was an overwhelming anxiety that the Germans would goose-step their way into town at any moment.

The Germans never did march into Witte. Instead, they came by air in the dark of night on May 10, 1940. It was the night before Andrew's twelfth birthday, and the van der Bijl family huddled together in stressful sleeplessness. Andrew's birthday was forgotten as the bombs began to drop on nearby towns, obliterating whole cities from existence. Within days, Holland surrendered to the Germans.

When the surrender was complete, the unstrategic town of Witte fell under the control of an overfed little German lieutenant and his handful of over-aged soldiers. Andrew saw an opportunity for revolt. He crept from his house in the darkest hour of the night and poured a bag of highly rationed sugar into the gas tank of the lieutenant's car. The villagers had to stifle their amusement when the car sputtered and stalled the next morning. Andrew felt like a hero.

As summer wore on, food in the cities began to dwindle. In small towns like Witte, however, family farms still had abundant produce. One sunny summer morning, Andrew loaded up a basket with cabbages and tomatoes and started out on the long walk to the town of Alkmaar. Just inside the city, he stopped at a little shop.

"Do you need some vegetables?" Andrew asked the busy shopkeeper. "I have some here for trade."

The shopkeeper turned, and his eyes widened at the large basket on Andrew's arm. He glanced around the shop, noting the largely empty shelves.

"How much?" the shopkeeper asked warily.

"No money," Andrew said, lowering his voice and stepping closer to the counter. "I want to trade. I hear you have some fireworks."

The shopkeeper's face relaxed into a smile. "I think I can help you," he said.

Andrew bartered boldly and had soon exchanged his basketful of produce for a basketful of fireworks.

He carefully laid the thick-stemmed flowers he had brought on top of his basket to conceal the fireworks.

"Thank you, sir," Andrew said as he turned to go.

"Wait," the shopkeeper called. He reached under the counter and pulled out the largest cherry bomb Andrew had ever seen. "Take this."

"But I have nothing left to trade," Andrew protested, trying to hide his excitement.

The shopkeeper came from behind the counter and tucked the cherry bomb into Andrew's basket.

"Hurry home," he urged, "or you'll be caught out past curfew."

Andrew grinned, thanked the shopkeeper, and hurried down the road. The miles flew by as Andrew walked and planned his attack. His heart raced with anticipation of all he would accomplish. This would be his greatest mission ever!

With bare feet and big plans, Andrew slipped from the house that night, disappearing into the shadows as soldiers patrolled the streets. When they had passed, Andrew scampered out of his hiding place and flew down the street to the grandest house in Witte—the house where the German lieutenant lived. He carefully placed the giant cherry bomb in the lieutenant's doorway and waited. As the patrolling soldiers drew near, Andrew lit the fuse and ran like the wind.

The soldiers screamed for him to stop as they drew their weapons. But Andrew zipped back and forth across the empty street. With an earthshaking BOOM, the cherry bomb exploded, distracting the soldiers and giving Andrew an avenue for escape. He darted through a yard and dove into a garden. The soldiers searched for an hour, but they couldn't find the skinny boy pressing himself into the dirt among the cabbages.

Emboldened by his successes, Andrew began launching daylight attacks, lobbing fireworks at passing soldiers and often barely escaping capture. But as the war dragged on and the German soldiers throughout Holland became more brutal, Andrew's escapades lost their appeal. Young men were forced to go into hiding or be sent to labor camps in Germany. Andrew's brother Ben went into hiding in the first months of the war, and the family did not hear from him for five years.

As Andrew grew older, the raids took younger and younger men. When he was just fourteen, Andrew began hiding with the other men and boys in the swampy polders whenever the military trucks rumbled into town. Everyone in the village was hungry, existing on boiled tulip bulbs and stagnant water. And when the Germans finally left after five long years, Andrew vowed he would never again allow others to oppress him. It was a vow that would shape his future in dramatic ways.

The Army Adventure

In the hazy heat of the summer of 1945, seventeen-year-old Andrew spent his days loitering, wandering aimlessly in the streets and enjoying the freedom of peacetime Witte. One warm afternoon, Andrew sauntered into the shady house and nearly ran over his little sister, Geltje.

"Papa wants to see you, Andrew," she announced. "You'll find him in the garden."

"Thanks," Andrew said, heading toward the back door.

"Andrew," Geltje said, a hint of warning in her voice, "he doesn't seem too happy."

Andrew rolled his eyes. He had a good idea how the conversation would go. He stopped in the doorway between the dim kitchen and the bright garden. Hesitancy pricked his heart and squeezed his stomach. He could see Papa hunching over his prized cabbages, gently and expertly uprooting weeds.

"I'm here, Papa," Andrew announced loudly, circling around to stand in front of his father.

23

Papa leaned back on his haunches, squinting up at Andrew. "Andrew," he shouted, "you are a man now."

"Yes, Papa." Andrew squirmed under Papa's stare.

"What are you going to do now? Do you have any plans for your life, Andrew?"

Andrew glanced past the house to the main street of town, sure that every neighbor and passerby could hear Papa's interrogation. He asked why Andrew had not pursued a career as a blacksmith or a machinist, both trades that Andrew had studied. Andrew had no good answers. Finally, Papa sighed and shook his head in frustration.

"Andrew, you must figure out what you want from life," he thundered. "Choose a career before the year ends."

Andrew slunk back into the house. He had no idea what he wanted from life. But he knew what he didn't want: to be a slave to his past, imprisoned in the tiny town of Witte, doing exactly what his father and his father's father had always done. He wanted something bigger, something better, more exciting, and filled with adventure. But he had no skills, no experience, and only a sixth-grade education. Where could that possibly take him?

Andrew slipped out of his klompen and out of the house. He began to run, down the street and out across the wide polders. His bare feet slapped the ground with a steady cadence, and the cobwebs began to clear from his brain. By the time he passed Alkmaar and hit the five-mile mark, a plan was beginning to form. And by the time he jogged back into Witte, sweaty and exhausted, he knew exactly what he wanted to do with his life.

As the family gathered by lamplight in the sitting room that night, Andrew took a deep breath and announced his intentions.

"I'm going to join the army."

Mama gasped unhappily, but Papa seemed pleased. He offered Andrew the use of his bicycle, and the following week Andrew rode to Amsterdam to enlist in the army. He soon discovered, however, that he was too young. The army would not allow him to join until 1946, when he would turn eighteen. But when that day arrived Andrew returned and successfully signed up as a soldier for the Dutch army.

After a brief stay back in Witte, Andrew reported to basic training. He worked hard and enjoyed every minute, finally feeling like he had found the adventure he had craved so long. On weekends, Andrew would walk to various churches in the nearby town of Gorkum. He barely tolerated the sermons, but he thoroughly enjoyed the inevitable dinner invitations from kind parishioners.

At a Reformed church service one Sunday, Andrew met Thile. She was gorgeous. "She's probably the prettiest girl I've ever met," Andrew reckoned. He was entranced by her raven hair, snow-white skin, and bright eyes. By the time he walked out the church door, Andrew had an invitation to dinner with Thile and her parents in their cozy apartment above her father's fishmonger shop near the docks. And before Andrew left that evening, Thile had promised to write to Andrew. He was sure Thile would become a very important person in his life.

In November 1946, Andrew said goodbye to Thile and his other friends in Gorkum. Then he went to Witte to say goodbye to his family before shipping out to Indonesia. Andrew proudly paraded through Witte in his uniform. The men clapped him on the back and the women smiled from a distance. Children danced around him, and Andrew held his head high.

In the familiar little family house, Andrew's siblings peppered him with questions. Papa embraced him with a bittersweet mix of pride and fear. But Mama grabbed Andrew's hand and pulled him into the quiet kitchen.

"Andrew, I want you to have this," she told him, slipping her well-worn Bible from beneath her apron.

"Yes, Mama."

She took his face in her hands and studied his eyes carefully. "I want you to promise me you'll read it, Andrew. In this book you will find all the answers you need to be happy in life. Will you read it?"

Andrew squirmed under the intensity of her gaze. "Yes, Mama."

She studied him a moment longer, and then pulled him close and squeezed him tightly. "Good boy."

Andrew's squad landed in Indonesia just at the end of 1946. In a couple of weeks it would be Christmas. Soon he and a select group of other soldiers were chosen to train as commandos. They spent long days under scorching sun on a small, secluded island, darting through obstacle courses, swinging over creeks, climbing over walls, and crawling under machine gun volleys. Andrew loved the thrill of practicing combat skills, the energy of the training, and the accomplished exhaustion of a full, frenzied day. He felt ready to fight.

After months of intense training, Andrew and his group were flown to the front lines, and Andrew's dream became a nightmare. The wonders of war didn't seem so wonderful anymore. Andrew found himself surrounded by pain, sorrow, darkness, and death. He saw things that terrified him, angered him, and broke his heart. He saw innocent people—young and old—dying on both sides of the battle, and his sleep was haunted with the horrors he had seen. It was not the adventure he had imagined.

For the next two years, Andrew became known for a bravery that bordered on insanity. He wanted to die. He wore a bright yellow straw hat into battle, daring the enemy to shoot him. And off the battlefield, he made bad choices too. Between missions, Andrew's life had become a blur of drinking, fighting, and reckless behavior. Mama's Bible lay forgotten in a trunk.

Feeling hopeless and alone, Andrew reached out to some of his pen pals, drafting long letters that expressed his heartache and confusion. Most of his acquaintances wrote sympathetic, detached, empty letters in return, filled with pretty words, but nothing that could help Andrew. Only Thile wrote letters that spoke to Andrew's heart. She wrote to him about guilt and forgiveness, awakening a spark of hope somewhere deep inside him. But then reality would crash down around Andrew, and the loneliness would engulf his soul again.

One afternoon, Andrew returned from a run, breathless and happy.

"Mail for you, Andy," his bunk mate announced.

"Thanks," Andrew said, crossing the room to his bunk. "Did you see who it was from?"

"Seemed like your brother," the bunk mate answered without looking up. "Bet you wish it was from that pretty girl in Gorkum instead."

Andrew laughed, flopped onto his bunk, and tore open the letter. It had been a long time since his family had written, and Andrew was hungry for news from home. But as he read Ben's words describing a funeral, Andrew suddenly realized it was Mama's funeral Ben was writing about. The telegram telling Andrew that Mama died had never been delivered. Andrew felt like he had been punched in the stomach. How could he ever go back to Witte without Mama's warm eyes and knowing smile to welcome him?

Andrew threw himself into his duties, overwhelmed by grief and lost in a pit of pessimism. He took long runs, but never felt like he could work hard enough or run far enough to escape his sadness. When news of a major drive against the enemy came down from headquarters, he felt a sense of relief.

On February 12, 1949. Andrew's unit went into battle at dawn, and he wore the yellow straw hat, more daring and defiant than ever. But his spirit and drive were gone. The adventure had lost all its allure.

A few days into the fierce battle, Andrew's unit walked into an ambush. Surrounded by the enemy on three sides, the soldiers were forced to run. Suddenly, Andrew fell to the ground. He tried to struggle to his feet, but he couldn't stand. When he looked down, he saw a bloody hole going straight through his right boot.

"I'm hit!" he cried out.

Then everything went dark.

Healing, Homecoming, and Heart Changing

When Andrew opened his eyes, a buddy was crouching over him, half pushing and half dragging him into a ditch.

"You're okay," his buddy kept saying, wild-eyed and frantic. "It's gonna be alright, Andrew. You're okay."

Andrew felt no anxiety, no pain, no fear—just the same relentless hopelessness that had plagued him for months. He pulled the sunshine-colored straw hat tighter onto his head and waited for the medics to come. When they finally arrived, Andrew insisted on wearing the very visible hat as they carried him off the field, through the thick of the battle. Andrew longed for death; he wanted to escape the darkness that pressed in around his soul.

A bullet zipped through his hat, millimeters from Andrew's head. Still, he refused to remove it. Hours later, just outside the operating room of the field hospital, a nurse approached him.

"Andrew van der Bijl?" she questioned, checking a clipboard of names.

"Yes, ma'am," Andrew answered.

"They are almost ready for you," she announced. "Let me just take your hat for you."

Andrew grabbed the hat fiercely and pulled it down hard. "No thanks," he hissed.

"But, soldier, there's a hole clean through it. And it will be in the way during surgery." She reached out and grasped the brim of the hat. "I'll keep it safe for you."

Andrew pulled the hat down even tighter and glared at the nurse, his eyes narrowing. A passing doctor gently grabbed the nurse's arm.

"Let him keep it," the doctor said, his voice low. "We'll work around it. It's practically a trademark of his unit. They say these boys have seen so many terrible things they've all lost their minds."

Andrew was taken into the operating room, yellow hat and all. Two-and-a-half hours later, he emerged. His foot was sewn up, but a gaping hole remained in both his hat and his heart.

Andrew's ankle had been shattered irreparably, and the doctors said he would never walk without a cane again. For a while, Andrew was distracted by the heavy plaster cast, the novelty of being wounded, and the visits from his buddies. Oddly enough, those same buddies who distracted Andrew did two things—with the best of intentions—that would change Andrew's life. First, after Andrew was injured, they went through his things and found an unmailed letter to Thile. It was a dark, depressing letter, filled with ugly truths about the war and the darkness in Andrew's life. It was a letter Andrew had never intended to actually mail, but his helpful buddies didn't know that. So they mailed it, and told him, and Andrew was sure he would never hear from Thile again.

The other thing Andrew's buddies found among his things was Mama's old Bible, shoved deep into the recesses of a duffle bag. A big, burly soldier brought the Bible to Andrew's room, cradling it awkwardly in his battle-blistered fingers.

"I, uh, thought you might want this," he said uncertainly.

Andrew shrugged and looked away, desperately trying to mask the pangs of longing and loneliness that shot through his heart. Memories of Mama reading that cherished Bible welled up and pressed against Andrew's eyelids. He didn't trust himself to speak, so he just shrugged again.

"Well, I'll just put it over here," the soldier said, laying the Bible on a bedside table. "It'll be there if you want it."

Weeks later the Bible was still untouched, but Andrew had a new distraction. He had taken to watching the nuns that staffed the hospital, and he could not comprehend their perpetual cheerfulness. They were always laughing and singing, even while changing bedpans, dressing wounds, bathing invalids, and doing all sorts of other unpleasant tasks. Finally, Andrew could stand it no longer.

"Why are you always so happy?" he asked one of them one day. "Why don't you complain about the awful tasks you have to do?"

The nun stopped and looked up, clearly surprised. "Why, Andrew," she said, "you must know the answer to that."

"Tell me," he begged.

"It is the love of Jesus Christ, of course," she answered, her eyes full of light. "That is why we do what we do, and that is how we do it so joyfully."

"I don't understand," Andrew muttered miserably.

The young nun studied him quizzically, her head tipped to one side. She glanced at the Bible on the bedside table, and then back at Andrew. After a long pause, she spoke.

"The answers you are looking for are there, Andrew," she promised, gesturing toward the untouched Bible. "They are all right there waiting for you."

With that she left the room, but her words stayed behind with Andrew. In the gathering gloom of evening, he reached out and grabbed the little Bible. He pulled it close to his face and flipped the first few fragile pages. Then he began to silently read the same ancient words Mama had faithfully followed with her life:

"In the beginning …"

Andrew drank in the words as fast as he could. Every day he read more and looked deeper. Although the stories were vaguely familiar, their truths hit him with new significance. He was particularly moved by the stories of Jesus in the gospels. His mind flooded with questions. And in the midst of his confusion, a letter arrived from Thile.

Thile had received and read Andrew's letter—the one he had never intended to send—and her heart was touched. She thought Andrew would find the healing he needed by studying God's Word. She included a short Bible study outline, which Andrew immediately began working on. Soon he and Thile were studying together through correspondence—Andrew in the makeshift field hospital in Indonesia, and Thile in the cozy apartment above her father's shop in Gorkum, Holland.

Hope was beginning to dawn in Andrew's heart, but the day his cast came off, the old pangs of bitterness and resentment swept away the budding hope. His shrunken, misshapen leg was a glaring reminder that his ability to run and his penchant for adventure had been taken from him forever. He began hobbling to the nearest bar every evening. The answers he had found were lost in the anger that overtook his heart.

On May 11, 1949—Andrew's 21st birthday—he boarded a ship and sailed for home. When he finally entered the tiny yard of the little house in Witte, Andrew was immediately entangled in embraces from his brothers and sisters. News was shouted, warm words whispered, tears cried, and new family members introduced. Andrew's sister Geltje was married, and Ben was engaged.

Into the hubbub came Papa, limping a bit himself. Tears of joy squeezed from the corners of his warm brown eyes.

"My boy!" he exclaimed joyfully in his half-shouting voice. "I am so glad you have finally come home."

One person was absent from the wonderful welcome: Mama. Andrew had known home would never be the same without her, but the ache was even deeper than he expected. Andrew's sister, Maartje, offered to take Andrew to Mama's grave. It was a long walk for his lame leg, but Andrew borrowed Papa's bicycle and flung the bad leg up over the seat. Then he half-hopped, half-rolled his way down the street.

Andrew shivered in the cemetery for an hour. When his questions were left unresolved, Andrew limped back home and into his old life.

Against all reason, Andrew soon found himself in the kitchen at the Whetstras' house. They chatted about current events and the fact that nothing ever really changed in Witte, and then Mr Whetstra looked Andrew in the eyes.

"Did you find what you were looking for, Andrew?" he asked.

"No, not really," Andrew admitted.

"We will keep praying for you," Mr Whetstra promised.

"Hmmph. A lot of good that will do," Andrew said bitterly. "In case you haven't noticed, I'm damaged. I'm broken. Nobody needs a crippled crusader who has to limp his way through his adventures."

His face was hot with anger and shame, and Andrew expected Mr Whetstra to reprimand him. Instead, Mr Whetstra smiled at Andrew and patted his shoulder.

"We will pray anyway," he insisted.

After seeing the Whetstras, Andrew went to see his old best friend, Kees. He was puzzled to find Kees at home, studying.

"What's gotten into you?" Andrew asked. "You used to hate studying."

"I've found my calling, Andrew. I know exactly what I want to do with my life."

"Lucky you," Andrew muttered. "So, what is this great life path?"

"I want to go into the ministry," Kees announced with pride. "Andrew, I'm going to be a preacher!"

Andrew struggled to mask the shock and mild amusement he felt. He could not imagine his best friend as a preacher. And he certainly did not want Kees to preach to him. But Kees seemed so certain of his choice. After they talked a while, Andrew left with a mixture of sadness, confusion, and curiosity churning inside him.

Since Witte seemed to hold no opportunities for Andrew, he reported to the veterans' hospital in Doorn for rehabilitation. He hated the exercises, the therapy, the poking and prodding, and even the encouragement. On his first weekend leave, Andrew took the bus to Gorkum to visit Thile.

She was beautiful—even more so than he remembered. As they sat by the wharf and talked, Andrew admitted he had stopped seeking God.

"Why?" Thile asked. "He hasn't stopped seeking you."

Andrew looked away. "What could God do with someone like me?"

Thile's ebony eyes danced. "Who knows?" she said. "Maybe something wonderful."

Andrew wasn't convinced. He left Gorkum that day feeling more distant from Thile than when he was in Indonesia. In fact, he felt distant from everyone. Feeling empty and useless, Andrew mechanically went through the motions of rehabilitating his body, but his soul cowered in the darkness that had become too familiar. He was surrounded by people, but he felt desperately alone.

Then, on a September morning in 1949, a pretty blonde girl stopped by the hospital to invite the soldier boys in rehabilitation to a tent meeting. The lewd band of soldiers heckled the girl, but nearly every one of them took the bus to the tent meeting that night. They huddled in the back of the giant tent, drunk and disruptive and disrespectful. But when the choir sang "Let My People Go," Andrew felt something snap in his spirit. He continued his inappropriate antics for the rest of the service, but he knew that he had unmistakably heard God's voice that night.

The next day, for reasons Andrew could not explain, he reached again for Mama's Bible and flipped it open.

The words and phrases leapt at him from the pages, almost alive and suddenly clear, as if the lens of love had brought God's Word into focus. Andrew found he could not tear himself away from the precious pages. The stories engaged him in a new way; the truths taught him like never before.

Within weeks, the Bible reading had grown to church attendance, first on Sundays, and then in neighboring towns nearly every night of the week. Andrew's family was amazed, then amused, and then alarmed. They could not understand the change that had overtaken his life.

There were those, however—Kees, his old teacher Miss Meekle, the Whetstras, and Thile—who not only understood, but also applauded the change. But as the weeks stretched into months, Andrew's fervor for his faith began to wear on even some of his staunchest supporters.

"Andy," Thile chided one day, "you are spending too much time and energy going from church to church and service to service. You'll get burnt out."

"I won't," Andrew insisted. "I just feel like there is so much more to discover, so much I need to learn."

"But Andy, you still don't have a job. Without a job, you have no future, and we have no future," Thile pleaded. "Don't you think you should spend more of your energy trying to find a job?"

Andrew shrugged. He understood Thile's concerns. Having no job was a problem. But he felt compelled to continue his journey to Jesus. He felt like he was very close to something very important.

A few weeks later, in the middle of January 1950, a brutal ice storm beat down on Witte. Andrew lay in the midnight darkness listening to the sleet crackling endlessly against the little house. The wind whispered and wailed to him with a thousand voices from his past. A million memories and a hundred emotions crashed together in that moment. And cowering beneath the covers, Andrew suddenly understood what he had to do.

"I am a sinner, God," he prayed aloud into the night. "I am wretched and damaged and hopeless. But I accept the death and resurrection of your Son. I ask you to forgive my sin and be Lord of my life."

Andrew thought of his dreams of adventure and his desires for fame and fortune. He knew these things came from his own heart, not from God. With a deep sigh, Andrew continued his prayer.

"God," he said, "I'm letting go of all my hopes and dreams. I want to do your will, not mine. Lord, if you will show me the way, I promise I will follow you. Amen."

It was a simple prayer, but when God opened Andrew's heart he began opening doors for Andrew. From that moment, Andrew's whole life began to change.

A Career and a Calling

Andrew woke the next morning with a heart full of joy. He felt like he had been given a new chance at getting life right. When he shared his experience, the Whetstras and Kees were thrilled. Kees invited Andrew to go to Amsterdam with him to hear a famous evangelist. They made the long trip together and found seats near the back of the auditorium. In the crowded room, the evangelist gave a stirring sermon. Then his eyes scanned the crowd.

"I've been feeling all night that something special is going to happen," he said. "I believe there is a young person here—probably a young man—who is about to be called to missionary service."

He stared out over the crowd again. Feeling uncomfortable, Kees and Andrew stood to slip out. When heads turned their way, they quickly sat back down. Then, as if in obedience to some unspoken command, Kees and Andrew stood again and made their way to the front of the hall. The evangelist welcomed them with joy and prayed over them. Then he asked them to stay after the service.

"Boys!" the evangelist exclaimed as he approached Andrew and Kees again a short time later. "Are you ready for your first assignment?"

Andrew and Kees exchanged worried, uncertain glances. They hadn't expected to have an assignment. Then again, they hadn't expected to come forward and surrender to missionary work during the service either.

"Here's what I want you to do," the evangelist continued. "What town do you boys come from?"

"Witte," Andrew and Kees said simultaneously.

"Excellent!" the evangelist replied. "I want you to go back to Witte and hold an open-air church service, right in the middle of town. I'll be there too, of course. First I'll speak, and then you'll each take a turn. How about this Saturday?"

Kees and Andrew were stunned and a little overwhelmed. Street preaching? In Witte? This Saturday?

"Yes, sir," they both muttered.

That Saturday, the entire town of Witte showed up for the open-air service. Andrew and Kees stood on a rickety, makeshift platform with the evangelist. When Andrew's turn came, his mouth was dry and his legs were rubbery. He couldn't remember a word of the sermon he had prepared. So he shared his story—the horrors of Indonesia, the discouragement of disability, and the peace of surrender on that stormy night.

Andrew read the effects of his words on faces he had known his whole life, and it empowered him.

Thile's response to this new adventure, however, was less enthusiastic.

"Oh, Andy," Thile said. "Maybe God does want you to do mission work. But the best mission work begins at home. Don't you think you should get a job for now and let that be your mission field?"

Andrew couldn't argue with Thile's logic. He asked his brother-in-law to put in a good word for him at the factory where he worked. Ringers' Chocolate Factory in Alkmaar was the biggest employer near Witte. Days later, Andrew was called to the hiring office.

Andrew squirmed anxiously on a narrow wooden bench outside the office at Ringers'. He was determined to get a job, but he had a nagging fear that no one would want to hire a cripple without any factory experience. But Andrew was hired and started that same day, counting boxes of chocolate, stacking them, and wheeling them to the shipping room. An errand boy led Andrew through the endless labyrinth of the factory hallways to a large room filled with nearly 200 girls packing boxes of chocolates.

As Andrew walked through the door, he was greeted by whistles and suggestive language. There was nothing ladylike about these factory girls. They were a crude, uncouth gang led by a brash, aggressive girl named Greetje. Andrew was totally unprepared for the foulness of these girls. He realized the factory was truly a mission field, but he felt ill-equipped to share Christ with the girls that surrounded him with evil.

One girl at Ringers' stood out from the rest. In the shipping room was a timekeeper's window where Andrew had to take receipts for the boxes he brought in. Behind the glass partition was a slender blond with warm, sparkling brown-green eyes. She was very young, but her smile was gentle and knowing.

"Don't mind the girls," she said. "They aren't all that bad. Mostly they just try to shock the newcomers. And today, that means you."

Andrew's cheeks flushed with gratitude. He studied the girl as she wrote up his next order. He felt like he knew her from somewhere, but he couldn't recall where. Too soon, the girl handed Andrew the new order and he headed reluctantly back to the packing area. But as the days passed, he found himself frequently visiting the timekeeper's window and even passing friendly little notes to the girl with the twinkling eyes and laughter in her smile.

"I'm worried about you, you know," Andrew told the girl after he had worked at Ringers' for a month "You're too young and too pretty to work with these girls."

The girl threw back her head and laughed, blond hair bobbing around her rosy cheeks. "They aren't that bad," she insisted. "Most of them just need friends. I believe Jesus sent me here to be a friend to these girls."

Andrew was surprised. He had a fellow missionary right in front of him! And he suddenly remembered where he had seen the girl before. She was the same girl who had come to the veteran's hospital to invite Andrew and his buddies to the revival meeting!

Nearly shaking with excitement, Andrew explained why he remembered her. He told her how the tent meeting changed his life, igniting his personal faith quest. He shared his calling to missionary work and why he had come to Ringers'. Then he asked the girl for her name.

"I'm Corrie," she said with a smile. "Corrie van Dam."

From that day on, Andrew and Corrie made it their mission to work together for Christ. They made it their aim to be like Jesus to their work colleagues—light in this spiritually dark world. They looked for girls with problems and personal challenges and tried to help. They took girls to revival services and tent meetings. One day, Andrew even invited the raucous ringleader, Greetje, to a weekend Bible conference. To his surprise, she agreed to come.

When the conference weekend was over and the bus dropped them back in Alkmaar, Andrew had an offer for Greetje, who lived one town over from Witte.

"Can I give you a ride home, Greetje?" Andrew asked. "I have a jump seat on the back of my bike, and I'm going your way. I could save you the bus fare."

Andrew could see Greetje mentally wrestling with the decision. Finally, she took Andrew up on his offer. She climbed onto the jump seat of the old bicycle, and they pedaled away.

Andrew had intended to confront Greetje with her need for Christ as soon as they got into the countryside. But he felt God telling him not to talk about religion at all. So they discussed the weather, the scenery, their childhood memories, and a dozen other topics. And when Andrew dropped Greetje at her street, she actually smiled and thanked him.

The next morning, Corrie ran up to Andrew as soon as he arrived at the factory. Her face was glowing.

"What did you say to Greetje yesterday?" she asked.

Andrew was puzzled by Corrie's enthusiasm. "I didn't say anything."

"Well, something is different," Corrie insisted. "She's not the same Greetje she was last week."

As the morning wore on, Andrew had to admit Corrie was right. Greetje was helping others and speaking kindly, and she didn't crack a single inappropriate joke all morning. At lunch time, Greetje brought her tray and sat next to Andrew.

"You surprised me yesterday," Greetje said.

"What do you mean?" Andrew asked.

"Well," Greetje began, "I expected you to try to force me to become a Christian on that long ride home yesterday. But you didn't, and it surprised me."

Andrew shrugged. "The timing just didn't feel right."

"I thought maybe you thought I was too much of a sinner for God to save," Greetje admitted, staring at her tray.

"Of course not," Andrew said. "If God can save me, God can save anyone."

Greetje brightened. "That's what I learned! Andrew, I prayed for the first time in a long time last night. I told God I knew I was a sinner, and I asked Him to forgive my sins. And then I told Him I wanted to start over again, if He would let me."

She paused and looked Andrew directly in the eyes. "Andy, I cried all night. But this morning, I felt reborn. I'm going to live for God, starting today!"

Andrew felt a strange mix of joy and relief. It was the first time he had watched God truly transform a life other than his own. As Greetje continued to grow in her new relationship with Christ, her transformation impacted her other coworkers. There was a revolution of sorts taking place in the factory, and Andrew—along with Corrie and Greetje—was on the front lines. But Andrew felt there was more he was supposed to be doing. Inside him, a war was raging—the battle between the comforts of home and the calling of God's Spirit. Andrew knew he had a choice to make, but he struggled desperately to find the courage to do what he knew he should do.

Sweet Surrender

Burdened by a calling he couldn't shake, Andrew confided in Thile that he was still determined to do missionary work. She saw his passion and determination, and she wrote to the mission board of her church, asking what it would take for Andrew to become a missionary. After reviewing Andrew's school records—including all the years he missed during the war—the church wrote back that Andrew would need twelve more years of schooling before he could be ordained as a missionary.

Twelve years felt like a lifetime, and formal schooling was an expense Andrew hadn't included in his budget. He half-heartedly enrolled in a few correspondence courses, but he struggled to believe this was God's path for him. By scrimping and saving, Andrew slowly acquired a tiny library of books to help with his schooling, and when his old teacher, Miss Meekle, offered to tutor him in English, Andrew eagerly accepted. As long as God was opening doors, Andrew promised himself he would walk through them and see where they led him.

One day after a particularly promising English lesson, Miss Meekle turned to Andrew with concern in her eyes.

"Andrew," she asked solemnly, "are you sure you need to go through twelve years of seminary training?"

Andrew shrugged. "I guess so. That's what the leaders of Thile's church say. Why?"

"Well, it's just that you're already twenty-four," Miss Meekle reasoned. "By the time you finish all this training, you'll be nearing forty. I just find it hard to believe God wants to wait that long to use you."

Andrew looked at Miss Meekle in surprise and then studied the floor. He had struggled with those same doubts over and over in his mind. To hear someone else express them out loud was like a confirmation of his concerns. He wondered if he was on the wrong path after all.

When he shared his spirit with an evangelist friend—the same one who had started Andrew on his missionary journey—the old evangelist just chuckled.

"You sound like one of those WEC people," he observed.

"WEC? What's that?" Andrew asked. "Is it another seminary? I've had about all I can take of school."

The evangelist chuckled again. "Nope," he said. "WEC is definitely not a traditional school. In fact, their feelings for traditional seminary are about the same as yours."

"So what do they do?" Andrew asked, his curiosity piqued.

"Worldwide Evangelization Crusade—that's what WEC stands for—is a group from England that sends missionaries out to areas where no church missions programs exist," the evangelist explained. "They have a short-term, two-year training program, and they teach their missionaries practical tasks and how to live by faith instead of relying on funding from churches."

Andrew wasn't sure about the concept of WEC. The reduced requirements for training appealed to him, but the thought of living by faith—and potentially in abject poverty—was less enticing. He shared his thoughts with Kees, who was already several years into his ordination training. To Andrew's surprise, Kees was immediately interested in WEC.

"In Matthew 10, Jesus told His disciples to go out without provisions, trusting God to provide," Kees recalled. "It sounds like a reasonable theory, definitely biblical. I'd love to learn more."

A few months later, a WEC representative named Mr Johnson visited Holland, and Andrew biked over to the city of Haarlem to meet him. His clothing was unmended and ill-fitting but Mr Johnson's description of the work of WEC was animated and impassioned. He told Andrew about the WEC training school in Glasgow, Scotland, and how it trained students in both pastoral and practical matters.

Andrew sped back to Witte and hurried to see Kees. Together they pedaled across the polders to question

Mr Johnson. Kees asked deep, demanding questions that betrayed his interest level. He seemed intrigued by Mr Johnson's answers. Within days, Kees had written to WEC, made application, and been accepted for admission.

Kees wrote often from the training center in Glasgow. Andrew was fascinated, but hesitant. He felt stupid due to his lack of schooling and useless due to his crippled ankle. Andrew wasn't sure if he wanted to be a missionary because it was God's will, or if he just wanted to be a missionary because it appealed to his sense of adventure. He wondered if God could really use someone with his limitations.

In September 1952, Andrew set out on a Sunday afternoon stroll across the polders near Witte. He was unsettled and uncertain about the direction of his life, and he knew he needed to seek God in a deep, undistracted way. He had always found it easiest to connect with God on the wide expanses of the polders, and as he walked, he began to pray out loud.

"God," he prayed, "You know I want to do your will. You know my heart. So why haven't you shown me the right path? Why can't I find your will?"

Silence engulfed Andrew, wrapping itself around him with the falling twilight. And in the silence, Andrew finally found his answer.

"Oh God," he prayed, dropping to his knees, "I haven't ever truly given you my whole life. You have my heart and soul, but I have always found excuses to avoid your callings. I've used my lack of education and my physical disabilities as ways to disconnect myself from your will. God, I'm so sorry."

With tears of sweet surrender trickling down his dusty cheeks, Andrew made a promise to God. He promised to do whatever God wanted him to do, in whatever way God wanted him to do it. No arguments. No excuses. Just obedience. Andrew promised God that his next step would be the first step on his journey to follow unconditionally.

As Andrew rose to his feet and took a step forward, searing pain shot through his crippled ankle. He cried out and fell back to the ground. Sucking in deep breaths, Andrew felt the pain begin to subside. After a few moments, he struggled to his feet again.

Andrew gingerly tested his weight on the bad foot. He felt no pain. He took one long step, then another. Still, there was no pain. His eyes wide with wonder, Andrew broke into a light jog, something he hadn't been able to do in years. Suddenly, Andrew understood what had happened: God had healed him! He wasn't crippled anymore!

That night, Andrew walked nearly four miles to an evening service in a nearby town. The next day, he walked all over the Ringers' Chocolate Factory. And the next week, Andrew formally applied to the WEC training school in Glasgow. Andrew knew it was time to begin his ultimate adventure at last.

Andrew was scheduled to leave for London in April 1953. On his last day at Ringers', Corrie—his faithful friend and fellow factory missionary—told him she was leaving too, headed for training to be a nurse. They wished each other well and said a quiet goodbye, each knowing God was preparing to use the other in mighty ways. And they each silently hoped their paths would cross again one day.

Thile was not nearly as happy for Andrew as Corrie had been. Instead, Thile and her family were downright resistant to Andrew going to WEC. Andrew figured they just needed some time and space to finally embrace God's plan for Andrew's life. But in early April, Andrew received a short, terse letter from Thile. She said she could not agree with or approve of his choices, and until he changed his path, she would prefer that he not write to her or visit her.

Andrew was stunned. He had planned to marry Thile someday, and now she wanted nothing to do with him, all because he was following God's will. Andrew knew he must choose God over Thile—it was his only real choice. But the pain of her rejection hurt more than anything he had ever known.

Two days after the heartbreaking letter from Thile, Andrew received another message. In a brief telegram, the London branch of WEC informed Andrew that upon reconsideration of his application and current enrollment numbers, Andrew's admission to the school in Glasgow was being revoked and denied. He was advised to reapply in a year.

Andrew had already sold nearly everything he owned to pay for his travel and tuition. He had already purchased a ticket to London for April 20th. So despite the closing doors and obvious obstacles, Andrew charged ahead, hearing in his heart a still, small voice saying, "Go."

The next day, Andrew packed his few remaining belongings, kissed his family, and boarded a bus for the first leg of his journey. When he arrived in London at the WEC building, Andrew sighed in relief. It was a large building, squatting on a little parcel of land. The paint was peeling, the shutters dangling, and the concrete steps crumbling, but Andrew felt strangely at home. He marched up to the front door and knocked enthusiastically.

The kind lady who opened the door could not understand Andrew's broken English, but she quickly found a man who could help them. He greeted Andrew in Dutch, and Andrew's face relaxed at the familiar words. Andrew introduced himself, and the man looked puzzled.

"I am familiar with your name," he apologized. "But we sent you a telegram days ago. There is no room for you in Glasgow this year. Didn't you receive our message?"

Andrew smiled. "Yes. I received it."

The man's brows drew together. "And you still came? Why?"

"When God's time is right, a place will open for me. I want to be right here so I am ready," Andrew said with assurance.

The man smiled broadly. "I believe you fit in with WEC already," he said. "I think we can let you stay here at headquarters for a bit, as long as you are willing to work and practice your English while you are here."

For two months, Andrew awoke every morning and had a quiet time in the garden, an English Bible in one hand and a dictionary in the other. The rest of his day was spent painting the massive building. Then he studied English until evening devotions, a time when the workers met together and took turns leading a little worship service.

Following Andrew's second time leading the service, a deep, jolly voice from the back of the room boomed out, "So, this is our Dutch boy! I think he gave a very fine sermon."

Andrew looked up to see a portly man with a large round head and blue eyes that sparkled with mischief. He was introduced as William Hopkins, and when Andrew greeted him, he took Andrew's thin hands and shook them vigorously. The WEC director explained that the time had come for Andrew to leave headquarters, and Mr Hopkins would help him get the necessary British working papers. Then Andrew could get a job.

"Gather your things," Mr Hopkins instructed, giving Andrew a friendly whack on the back. "You're coming home with me tonight!"

As Andrew packed his few belongings, a WEC worker filled in some details about Mr Hopkins. He was a highly successful London contractor, but he lived with no luxuries and very little human comforts because he constantly gave away all his money to those in need. He was also skilled at securing work permits and jobs for needy students. He was never one to turn away a poor, lost soul, and he lived his life as much like Jesus as possible.

Andrew said goodbye to the WEC staff and climbed into Mr Hopkins' truck. Soon they arrived at the warm, tidy little cottage along the Thames River where Mr Hopkins lived with his wife, who was chronically ill and spent most of her time in bed.

"Welcome, Andrew," Mrs Hopkins said with a warmth that made him instantly miss his mother. "We're so glad you're here. Please make yourself at home. Everything we have is yours."

"Thank you, ma'am," Andrew said, overwhelmed by the kind spirit he sensed in both Mr and Mrs Hopkins.

"I do have to warn you though," Mrs Hopkins went on, her eyes twinkling with amusement as she looked at Mr Hopkins. "My dear husband is notorious for bringing in strays. So if you should come home one night and find a poor drunkard in your bed—and that will likely happen at some point—just grab some of the extra pillows and blankets in the living room here and make yourself a bed by the fire."

Within a week, Andrew saw her words come to life. He watched Mr and Mrs Hopkins repeatedly trust God to provide when they reached out to a needy soul. Best of all, Andrew saw that God never failed them, even when provision seemed impossible. Watching them live their faith strengthened Andrew's faith.

Although Andrew expected to stay with the Hopkins for only a few days, his work permit was repeatedly denied. To keep busy, Andrew found chores to do around the house—mopping, laundry, ironing, cooking, and whatever else needed to be done. Mr and Mrs Hopkins were so touched by his attention to their needs, they asked him to stay. He became their cook, housekeeper, and errand boy, and they soon became an English mother and father to him. Andrew called them Uncle Hoppy and Mother Hoppy, and he grew to know and love them dearly.

Then one day a letter came from Glasgow! Andrew was accepted for admission to the WEC training center. With tears that were tinged with both joy and sadness, Uncle Hoppy, Mother Hoppy, and Andrew celebrated. Then preparations were made for travel to Glasgow. In September 1953, Andrew said goodbye to his dear friends and left London, certain that his truest and greatest adventure was on the brink of beginning.

The Cry of the Communists

Andrew arrived at the dormitory in Glasgow with a healthy dose of enthusiasm, tempered only slightly by mild apprehension. His few fears fled, however, when Kees greeted him at the door, throwing it open and practically pulling Andrew inside.

"Brother!" Kees exclaimed. "I am so glad you are finally here!"

After several joyous minutes of greeting and catching up, Kees showed Andrew to his room and introduced him to the other students. Kees gave Andrew a rundown on the rules and regulations. Then it was time to meet the director, Steward Dinnen.

"Our primary purpose here, Andrew, is to teach our students to trust God," Mr Dinnen said. "We want our missionaries to be flexible, to be well-equipped, and to go wherever God might send them. Do you understand?"

"Yes, sir," Andrew answered solemnly. "That is exactly why I am here."

"Good," Mr Dinnen said with a smile. "We believe less in general education and more in guided experience. We want our students to learn to trust God completely and unconditionally. We firmly believe the will of God will never lead us where the grace of God will not supply us."

This conversation was the cornerstone of two years of incredible experiences for Andrew. There were highs and lows, days of fearless faith, and nights of gnawing doubt. But through it all, Andrew learned to know God deeper, trust Him more, and rely on Him completely. It was a time of learning and growth like nothing Andrew had ever known before.

Near the end of the first semester, the time came for the first evangelism training trip.

"You're going to enjoy this experience, Andy," Mr Dinnen promised as the date of the trip drew nearer. "It is a true faith exercise. Each team member is given a one-pound banknote. Your team must take a missions tour throughout Scotland, paying for lodging, transportation, hall rental, food, advertising, and anything else you might need."

"All with one pound?" Andrew was incredulous. "Seems impossible."

"With men, maybe; but with God …" Mr Dinnen grinned broadly. "And it gets even better. You must sustain yourselves for four weeks, and when you return, you must give us all the money back."

"Give it back?" Andrew shook his head. "You must be joking."

"Not at all. In fact, this exercise in faithfulness has proven successful time and time again."

Andrew chuckled. "Well, I guess we'll have to take up offerings regularly."

Mr Dinnen smiled again. "Oh, no," he said. "You are not allowed to take up any offerings. In fact, you are never allowed to speak of money at all, except within your team. If you ever ask for help with your needs—monetary or otherwise—you will have failed the experiment. If people give to you on their own, you may use the money, but you must never express a need."

For his evangelism tour, Andrew was on a team with four other young men. As the four weeks progressed, he was repeatedly astounded by the way God provided. A young man's parents would send a letter with a little money. A church they had visited days or even weeks earlier would send a check. A local farmer would share an abundance of produce.

One day, near the end of the trip, the team was holding meetings in Edinburgh. A large group of young people had come to the service, and the team was especially burdened to reach them. Without any consultation or planning within the group, one team member stood up and addressed the large group of youngsters.

"Tomorrow evening, before the service," he announced, "we would like you all to join us here for tea at four o'clock. Who will come?"

Two-dozen hands went up. The team members were instantly a bit panicked. They were penniless, having used their last money to rent a hall for their services.

In fact, they were so penniless that they were sleeping on the floor of the hall. They owned only five cups and had no food to serve at tea. But they had learned that where God gave a prompting, He also made provisions.

Several young people offered to help with the tea, volunteering milk, sugar, and dishes. One essential ingredient was missing, however—the cake. That night, the team huddled in their blankets on the floor of the large, empty hall.

"Lord," one prayed aloud, his voice echoing in the darkness, "here we are again in a tight spot. We know you brought us here. And we know you'll walk us through."

Another took up the prayer. "From somewhere, God, we need a cake. Will you please help us, like you have so many times before?"

The young men fell asleep wondering how God would meet their need for cake. The morning brought no answers. The mail came with no unexpected funds. The tables were set. The water was boiling. The need was about to go unmet. Then, at precisely 3:45 pm, the doorbell rang.

"Our delivery day is over," said the young postman who stood at the door, "but this package seemed like food, and I hate to let food sit overnight. So I thought I'd bring it by on my way home."

He held out a large box addressed to Andrew from Mother Hoppy in London. As soon as the postman left, Andrew carefully tore open the package. Inside was a huge, delicious, glistening chocolate cake!

Andrew continued his miracle-laced life through the rest of his schooling. He always received an unexpected check just when he needed it most; always found unexpected blessings when his spirit was wearing thin; always noticed supplies unexpectedly lasted longer than he hoped.

These lessons in trust and provision carried Andrew through to the week before graduation. One quiet morning in the spring of 1955, Andrew went to the dormitory basement to retrieve his suitcase. He would soon head back to Witte to seek God's will for his life. As he reached for the suitcase, Andrew saw a magazine he had never seen before sitting atop a dusty box.

He picked up the magazine. It was full of glossy pictures of crowds of enthusiastic young people marching in the streets of Peking and Prague, Warsaw and East Berlin. It was Communist propaganda, although it never actually mentioned Communism. Near the back of the magazine was an announcement for a youth festival planned for Warsaw in July. The announcement was an open invitation for anyone who wanted to attend.

Deep in his soul, Andrew felt an inexplicable stirring. He knew God wanted him to go to that festival, although he did not understand why. So, in the spirit of obedience that had become so familiar to him, Andrew wrote to the Warsaw address in the announcement. He told the organizers he was a Christian missionary in training, and he would love to attend the festival just to exchange ideas. In no time at all, Andrew received a response telling him he was welcome to come. Enclosed were all the appropriate identification documents and arrangements to travel on a train leaving from Amsterdam.

After graduation, Andrew made a quick visit to Witte. Then, on July 15th, 1955, Andrew travelled to Amsterdam and boarded a train to Warsaw, Poland. The train was packed with young people—men and women in their teens and twenties with open minds and eager hearts, hungry for the bright future promised in the propaganda. The sheer number of people stunned Andrew.

He clung to his suitcase. It was heavy, but there were only a few items of clothing inside. The rest of the space was full of booklets and tracts proclaiming the gospel. The Communists had an abundance of literature to win over the young attendees. Andrew was determined to use the same tactics to reach their searching hearts for Christ. He wasn't sure if it would work, but he knew he had to try.

In Warsaw, Andrew found his "hotel" was nothing more than an old school that was converted into living accommodation for hundreds of festival visitors. After checking in, Andrew decided to explore the city. He boarded a bus and watched the buildings whiz past. All around him were voices, chattering away in Polish. How could he reach people for Christ when he couldn't even say hello in their language? He decided to try

German, since he had heard some Poles spoke at least a little German.

Andrew stood and pushed his way into the narrow aisle of the bus. He steadied himself against the rickety seats as the bus swayed around a sharp corner.

"I am a Christian," he announced in German. "I have come all the way from Holland to meet Polish Christians. Can you help me?"

The voices all stopped at once. No one stood. No one spoke. No one responded to Andrew's question, although he was quite sure many of them had understood what he was asking. Feeling a little foolish and frustrated, Andrew settled back into his seat.

A few stops down the line, a peasant woman passed Andrew's seat and whispered an address in German and added, "Bible shop." Then she was gone.

With the help of a handful of strangers, Andrew found the Bible shop. The doors were padlocked and heavy bars covered the windows, but Andrew could clearly see the assortment of Bibles inside. A notice was pasted to the front door. When Andrew finally found someone to translate the message, he learned the shopkeeper was on vacation until July 21st.

Andrew breathed an impatient sigh and wandered back to his hotel. He could hardly wait until July 21st. He felt the Bible shop was an important stop along his journey through God's will. Andrew felt like he was on the verge of something big, something life-changing. But even Andrew couldn't imagine what God had in store.

A God of Great Gifts

As the festival wore on and July 21st drew nearer, Andrew and his fellow visitors were shown the best and brightest of what Communist Poland had to offer. Every tour was carefully orchestrated so festival participants would only develop positive associations. These day trips were pleasant, but Andrew wondered what he would find if he ventured out on his own, traveling to parts of the city and talking to groups of people that weren't being proudly presented.

One morning, Andrew rose at dawn and slipped out into the city before the rest of his group awakened. What he saw was dramatically different from the rose-colored tours. Bombed out buildings stood like crumbling sentinels. In their shadows, ragged men, women, and children in tattered clothes stood in long lines for scarce bits of food. Whole families lived in makeshift shelters carved out of the pockmarked basements of building rubble. Dirt, drunkenness, and despair were everywhere. Andrew felt desperate to save these lost, empty souls.

He wandered back to the hotel and tried to smile as he joined the group on a tour the next day. But he couldn't deny the stark differences between what he was being shown and what he had discovered on his own. He couldn't forget what he had seen.

When Sunday came, the festival organizers planned a massive demonstration at the national stadium. Once again, Andrew slipped away. He was determined to find Polish Christians. If there was still a Bible shop, there had to be a Christian church somewhere. With the help of a friendly taxi driver and a whole lot of pantomiming and hand signals, Andrew found himself across Warsaw, sitting in his first church service behind the Iron Curtain of Communism.

Andrew was surprised to see the church mostly full, and the singing and preaching seemed enthusiastic and joyful, although he couldn't comprehend the Polish language. After the service, Andrew lingered in the foyer, hoping someone who spoke one of his languages would approach him. He desperately wanted to know more about how a church could freely operate in the realm of a godless government.

"Welcome to our church," a voice said in English, directly behind Andrew. "What brings you here, friend?"

Andrew turned and saw the pastor. "I am a Christian from Holland," Andrew explained with a smile. "I came to find out what God is doing in the lives of Polish Christians. May I ask you some questions?"

"Certainly," the pastor said. "As soon as the rest of the congregation leaves, I will be happy to speak with you."

Minutes later, Andrew found himself seated in a tidy office with the pastor and a handful of young people.

"Can you worship God openly and freely?" Andrew asked.

"For the most part," the pastor answered.

"As long as we stay away from political topics," a young man added, and several heads bobbed in agreement.

"Are any members of your church also members of the Communist Party?" Andrew wondered.

"Of course," said a girl. "Nearly everyone is these days."

"But they believe so many things that are contrary to God's Word," Andrew protested.

The pastor shrugged. "Sometimes we must compromise our beliefs for the greater good, you see? We give up some of our ideas, and they offer us freedom to worship."

Andrew's heart was heavy. He wasn't sure they could really claim freedom to worship when it meant rejecting parts of the Word of God. He was silent, unsure what to ask next.

"What type of church do you attend in Holland?" a young man asked.

"A Baptist church," Andrew answered.

"Would you like to go to a Baptist service while you are here in Poland?" the young man offered. Andrew nodded eagerly, and the young man jotted down an address. "There's a service tonight," he told Andrew.

The congregation at the Baptist church was smaller, older, and more ragged. As soon as they realized a foreigner was in their service, they asked Andrew to speak to them. He agreed somewhat reluctantly. With a German-speaking woman translating for him, Andrew preached the first of thousands of sermons behind the Iron Curtain. It was a simple sermon, but it was a profound experience for Andrew.

At the end of the message, the pastor stood and said, "Thank you for being here. Even if you had not spoken to us, we are blessedly reminded that we are not alone in our struggle."

Finally the 21st of July arrived, and Andrew made his way to the little Bible shop. When the shopkeeper arrived promptly at nine o'clock, Andrew eagerly introduced himself. To his great surprise, the shopkeeper just grunted in reply and seemed completely disinterested. When the shop was set up for the day, the shopkeeper went through the motions of showing Andrew around the shop, highlighting the wide variety of Bibles available in the assorted price ranges.

All morning, Andrew and the shopkeeper talked. It seemed the Bible was freely available, and the little shop was busy enough, but there was an underlying tension and unspoken fear that ran through every exchange. Andrew began to suspect the religious freedom he was observing was as false as the beautiful buildings and clean-scrubbed citizens he had seen on the organized tours. He felt the true religious landscape looked more like the bombed-out wastelands he had discovered on his private sojourns—full of hopelessness and despair.

The morning of his departure, Andrew slipped out of bed and into the dewy dawn. He sat on a bench on a lonely street corner, praying for each person he had encountered on his trip. As the sun rose higher and he neared the end of his prayers, Andrew heard music in the distance. Along the street came the Parade of Triumph, designed to conclude the festival. Thousands of young people marched through the streets, rank upon rank, singing and shouting. The sight was both energizing and terrifying to Andrew.

"God," he silently cried, "what good am I against so many? What difference can my little light make in the face of such darkness?"

As if in answer to his question, a breeze ruffled the pages of the little Bible that lay open in Andrew's lap. He put his hand on the pages to keep them from ruffling. Then he looked down. His fingers were resting on Revelation 3:2. He quietly read the verse out loud.

"Be watchful, and strengthen the things which remain, that are ready to die."

With sudden certainty, Andrew knew exactly what God was telling him to do. He was being called to spend his life ministering to struggling believers behind the Iron Curtain, lifting up the faithful and reaching those still entrenched in the darkness of Communism. It was a huge task, and in 1955 there was not a single foreign missionary doing work in the vast Communist mission field. But Andrew knew better than to deny God's call. Instead, he answered with the words of the prophet Isaiah.

"Okay, Lord," Andrew prayed. "Here I am. Send me."

When Andrew's train hissed into the station in Amsterdam, he felt drawn to visit the Whetstras, who had recently moved there. They joyfully welcomed him and showed him their large new house and light blue Volkswagen. Then they asked about the trip to Poland.

Andrew shared his experiences, one by one, with the captivated Whetstras. His heart was heavy with his burden for the hopeless, helpless people he had encountered. He expressed his burden to his friends.

"This is what God wants me to do," Andrew insisted.

He told the story of the wind in the Bible pages and his certainty of God's call.

"But I still don't see what one man can do against such a vast need," Andrew finished.

Mr Whetstra reluctantly agreed. "I don't know what strength can undertake a mission work like that."

"Why, no strength at all!" Mrs Whetstra exclaimed. She stood in the doorway, hands on her hips, shaking her head. "Andrew, you must know by now it is in our moments of weakness that God's strength flows through us. True, you do not have the strength to do this. But God does! And what greater strength could you ask for?"

With that empowering thought in mind, Andrew returned to the little house in Witte. When he arrived, he learned the family had all given up some precious space in the tiny dwelling and had given Andrew a room of his own to use as his headquarters. It was more than he could have hoped for. With a thankful heart, Andrew settled into his new space and waited for God's direction.

Within a week, invitations began to arrive for speaking engagements throughout the countryside. Andrew accepted every invitation. In 1955, everyone wanted to know about the mysterious world behind the Iron Curtain. Andrew was happy to share his heart with them. He hoped God would reveal His next direction at one of these meetings.

God did not disappoint Andrew. One day while speaking at a church in Haarlem, Andrew looked out at the standing-room-only crowd and noticed a group of Communists huddled in a back corner. He recognized some of them from the trip to Poland. He expected them to heckle him, but they listened silently to the presentation and the open question session afterward. When the crowd began to clear out, a few members of the group finally approached him.

"I didn't like your speech," a sharp-faced woman told him.

Andrew smiled. He recognized her as one of the group leaders on the Warsaw festival trip.

"I'm sorry," Andrew said kindly. "I didn't expect you to like it. But I spoke the truth about my experiences."

"That was not the truth!" She spat the words angrily. "You only told part of the story. Clearly, you have not traveled widely enough."

Excitement began to build in Andrew. "What do you mean?" he asked.

"You must visit more countries and travel throughout the Communist regime. You must meet more people," she insisted. "You must meet our leaders. Then you will understand."

Andrew could barely breathe. "How do you propose I do that?"

"It's quite simple, really," the lady said with a condescending smile. "I am in charge of selecting fifteen Dutchmen to represent Holland on a four-week trip to Czechoslovakia. I would like you to come and represent the voice of the churches."

Andrew breathed a silent prayer for wisdom. He also prayed if the trip were God's will, he would be able to go without cost.

"Thank you," Andrew said, "but I am afraid I will not be able to afford the travel costs."

"Well," the woman said, frowning. "For you, no charge."

Andrew grinned. "I'm in. When do we leave?"

The trip to Czechoslovakia was remarkably similar to the trip to Poland. The group was smaller, and the tours were more focused, so Andrew found it harder to sneak away on his own. The tour guides often spoke directly to Andrew, stressing the religious freedoms enjoyed under Communism. In fact, one tour guide told Andrew a group of scholars had just completed a new translation of the Bible into the Czech language.

When Andrew asked to meet the scholars, he was taken to an impressive facility. Somber men in black coats sat behind large desks piled high with papers. Andrew was shown a well-worn manuscript for the new Bible translation.

"The new translation has not been published yet?" Andrew asked one of the scholars.

He shook his head sadly. "Not yet. It has been ready for several years, but ..."

He looked at the tour guide who scowled back at him. The scholar studied the floor, his sentence unfinished.

"Are there older translations available for people to use while they wait for the new Bible?" Andrew wondered.

With a fearful glance toward the tour guide, the scholar took a step toward Andrew. Their faces were only inches apart.

"There are no Bibles for the people," he admitted, his voice barely above a whisper. "Bibles are very difficult to find."

The tour guide glared at the scholar, who stepped back quickly and hurried away to his desk.

"We're done here," the tour guide snapped. "Let's go."

He practically pulled Andrew through the door. They returned to the hotel in silence, but the damage had been done. Andrew had seen the truth.

On the last day of the trip, Andrew was desperate to investigate things on his own. It was Sunday, and he longed to find Czechoslovakian Christians and worship with them. But his group was scheduled to take a tour of the countryside, and it wasn't optional.

Andrew boarded the bus with a careful plan in his mind. At a stoplight in downtown Prague, while everyone else was focused on surveying the city sights, Andrew slipped through a narrow opening in the back door of the bus. As the tour bus pulled away without him, Andrew felt freedom wash over him. Within a half hour, he stood in front of a church he had spotted on a previous tour.

Andrew watched people enter, and as the service began, he slipped in and took a seat in the back. With surprise, he noted the handful of people with hymnals held high and at arm's length. When the preaching began, the few Bible owners did the same with their Bibles, holding them high. With slight shock, Andrew realized the people were sharing. There were only a dozen or so hymnals and Bibles to go around in the large congregation, so those who had them were sharing with those who did not. Andrew's heart ached as he watched men and women literally struggle to get closer to God's Word.

After the service, Andrew introduced himself to the pastor. They talked for hours, and the pastor explained the Communist persecution of the church in Czechoslovakia. The government selected all theological students. The government required pastors to renew their licenses every two months, and these applications were routinely denied. In addition, every sermon had to be written out word-for-word and approved by authorities before it could be preached.

As the time drew near for the afternoon service, the pastor had an idea.

"Would you speak in our service?" he asked.

"Am I really allowed to preach here?" Andrew wondered.

The pastor grinned. "Ah, see, I never said 'preach.' You are not allowed to 'preach' in Czechoslovakia. But you can bring us greetings from Holland." He paused. "And if you brought us greetings from the Lord, that would be okay too."

So, with the help of an interpreter, Andrew spent a few minutes "bringing greetings" to the church from Holland and the West. Then—for the next half hour—he "brought greetings" to the church from Jesus Christ. It was a marvelous experiment that went so well, Andrew and his new friends decided to repeat it. That day, Andrew "brought greetings" in five different churches. Each church was different, but each congregation was hungry for the Word of God and the knowledge that they were not alone in their struggle.

At the last church he visited, Andrew experienced the truest picture of the struggles of the church under the thumb of the Communist regime. It was already dark outside, and Andrew was hesitant to visit another church. He knew his tour group would be looking for him, and he didn't want to create trouble for himself or others. But Antonin, the young medical student who was his interpreter, begged Andrew to visit one last church that was in dire need of encouragement. Andrew reluctantly agreed.

When they arrived, the church was full, largely with young people. They peppered Andrew with questions about what it was like for Christians living in the West.

"Can Christians hold jobs in Holland?" one young man asked.

"Do they report you to the government if you attend church?" asked another.

"Can you still go to the university if you are a believer?" a girl wondered.

Andrew was puzzled by the questions until Antonin explained to him that in Czechoslovakia, being a Christian was considered direct opposition to the government. Antonin told Andrew that people often lost their jobs, educational opportunities, family, and even land and belongings, simply because they chose Christ over Communism.

After the last service, Antonin dropped Andrew at the hotel, and Andrew found himself wondering how he would find his tour group. He hoped he would not be in trouble, but for the sake of what had been accomplished that day, he was willing to endure a reprimand. When he didn't find the group at the hotel, Andrew wandered down to a restaurant where the group had eaten several times.

"Have you seen the group from Holland this evening?" Andrew asked the headwaiter.

"No, sir," he replied. "They did not eat here tonight. In fact, I have not seen them all day. Would you like me to get you something to eat?"

Andrew nodded and ordered a sandwich. Just as he took his first bite, the tour director thundered into the room, screaming at Andrew in Dutch. She threw some money on the table and pulled Andrew toward the door. Outside was a sleek, black government car. The limousine driver was massive and stone-faced. He ushered Andrew and the tour director into the car and locked the door behind them.

"Where have you been?" the tour director asked with ice in her voice. "We have searched everywhere—hospitals, police stations, even the morgue. You have delayed our group and inconvenienced everyone."

"My apologies," Andrew said. "I got separated from the group, so I spent the day traveling throughout the city. I did not mean to cause anyone any trouble."

He did not tell the tour director that the separation from the group had been intentional. He did not share the fact that his traveling had involved visiting and speaking at churches around the city. He smiled politely and waited for the inevitable consequences of his actions.

The tour director was not moved by Andrew's sincere apology. "You should know that you are no longer welcome in Czechoslovakia. Your visa is being immediately revoked. You will not be allowed to enter this country again," she finished coldly.

The car sidled up to the curb in front of the hotel. The silent chauffeur let Andrew and the tour director out of the car. The next day, Andrew left Czechoslovakia with his group. He later discovered the tour director had not been bluffing. His visa was revoked and future visa applications to Czechoslovakia were quickly denied. It would be quite some time before Andrew set foot in that country again.

Back in his little headquarters in Holland, Andrew wondered what his next step should be. He applied for visas to several countries, but was always held up by official processes and procedures. The wheels of the work to which he felt called seemed to be barely spinning, and Andrew was feeling impatient. Finally, he decided to accept an invitation from a Dutch magazine to write some articles about his journeys.

Within weeks after the articles were published, letters and donations from all over Holland began to pour into the magazine offices. These donations funded small projects that Andrew was undertaking while waiting for further direction. He was able to help with household expenses, replace his own worn-out coat, and mail a Czech Bible to Antonin. More important than the financial donations, however, were the promises of prayer.

Through his magazine articles, Andrew came to know Karl de Graaf, leader of a prayer group in the town of Amersfoort. This prayer group would meet for hours, seeking the voice of God. Andrew kept in touch with Karl, and was startled to find him at the door of the little house in Witte one day.

"Welcome, Karl," Andrew said warmly. "What brings you here?"

"I have come to teach you to drive," Karl announced.

"Why do I need to know how to drive?" Andrew questioned. "There is virtually no chance that I would ever be able to afford a car."

"Andrew," Karl said patiently. "I learned long ago not to argue with God's direction. He didn't tell me why you needed to learn to drive. He just told me to come and teach you. So here I am."

With that, Karl strode to his waiting car, and Andrew meekly followed. Week after week, Karl returned for more lessons. Andrew did not understand the logic behind learning to drive, but he worked hard and soon passed his driving test on the first try. He tucked his license in his pocket and continued on with his normal life, without even a bicycle—let alone a car—for transportation. Little did Andrew know, miracles were looming on the horizon!

The Miracles Multiply

Towards the end of 1956, the Hungarian Revolt brought hundreds of thousands of refugees flooding from Communist countries into the West. Most of these were immediately herded into massive camps along the borders. The largest camps were in West Germany and Austria. The call came out for volunteers to help in these camps, and Andrew was on the first bus out of Holland.

When he arrived at the camps, Andrew's heart was broken by what he saw. Dozens of people lived in tiny, shack-like houses, crammed in together in unthinkable squalor. There was not enough of anything—space, food, clothing, dignity. People were desperate and hopeless, struggling to stay together and make it through each day.

In addition to offering physical help, Andrew held prayer services, and it was in these services he discovered many of the younger people who had grown up under Communism had never seen a Bible and never heard the story of God's love. Driven to change that fact, Andrew established Bible classes to help fill the empty days of hopeless people with the ultimate message of hope in God. He watched lives be transformed and a sense of pride and belonging be restored.

As Andrew watched the transformative power of God's Spirit in the camps, his heart was thankful. But he wondered how many hundreds of thousands—millions, even—were left behind in the Communist countries with no knowledge of God's love, His sacrifice, and His desire for a relationship with them. He knew the work in the camps was important, but he felt compelled to go beyond the camps, behind the Iron Curtain, and into the very heart of the lies that were deceiving so many.

While he awaited God's direction, Andrew worked tirelessly, helping as many people as he could. One afternoon, after a particularly exhausting day, Andrew received a telegram informing him that Papa had died while working in his garden. Andrew swallowed the lump that immediately rose in his throat. He could see Papa's bent form, coaxing the plants gently from the earth. He could hear Papa's booming voice, welcoming him, chiding him, teasing him. With a heart bursting with memories and sadness, Andrew took the next train back to Witte.

The funeral was small and somber, and Papa was buried in the same grave as Mama in the tiny Witte cemetery. Within days, Andrew headed back to West

Germany and attacked his work with new vigor. He worked to get children into Holland, hoping to give them a better life, but they were repeatedly rejected for health reasons. Some of the refugees had lived in the camps for over a decade—since the end of World War II—and many had tuberculosis and other pandemic diseases that routinely swept through the crowded camps.

There was no real hope for the future among these lonely, lifeless people. All Andrew could offer them was the promise of God's love and care. Each day, Andrew sought God in a quiet time, asking for strength and wisdom and patience and joy so he could adequately represent God in the face of emptiness. He was determined to stay busy in the camps until God opened a new door.

One day, Andrew was summoned to the Yugoslavian consulate in West Berlin, near the camp where he was working. His Yugoslavian visa had been repeatedly denied, and Andrew assumed this time would be no different. But when he approached the clerk's window, Andrew received a thrilling surprise.

"Congratulations, sir," the clerk said with a wide smile. "Your visa has been granted. Enjoy your trip to Yugoslavia!"

Andrew grinned back as he took his paperwork from the clerk. Overwhelmed by good news and God's faithfulness, Andrew telephoned Mr Whetstra in Amsterdam. He had to share with someone!

"Good day, Mr Whetstra! This is Andrew van der Bijl," Andrew said when Mr Whetstra answered the telephone.

"Hello, Andrew," Mr Whetstra said warmly. "I thought you were in Berlin."

"I am," Andrew said, "but I have wonderful news and I just had to share it with someone. My visa to Yugoslavia got approved this afternoon! I'm finally going to be able to go behind the Iron Curtain as a missionary!"

"Praise God," Mr Whetstra exclaimed, a smile in his voice. "I guess you had better come here for your keys."

Andrew was confused. "Keys?"

Mr Whetstra laughed. "Yes, Andrew. Your keys. Mrs Whetstra and I talked it over, and we want to give you our Volkswagen. We decided months ago that when your visa finally came through to go behind the Iron Curtain, we would give you our vehicle to use in your ministry. No strings attached."

"But, sir . . ." Andrew was stunned.

"Don't even try to talk us out of it," Mr Whetstra advised. "We are obeying God's direction, and nothing you could say will change our minds. So, come pick up your keys!"

It all made sense now. The driving lessons from Karl were in preparation for the biggest gift Andrew had ever received. As he drove out of Amsterdam in the nearly new Volkswagen, registered in his name, Andrew felt an overwhelming sense of gratitude. God was already way ahead of him, supplying the needs for his work.

Andrew planned to leave for Yugoslavia in March 1957. He spent hours scouring Amsterdam for Bibles and gospel booklets in Yugoslavian languages. He worked out places to hide materials in the car so he could effectively smuggle them into the country, where they were forbidden. When he had worked out all of the minor details, Andrew waited for God to do the major work: providing money for travel and additional supplies.

Just before he hoped to leave, Andrew traveled to see Karl de Graaf. He wanted to show him the miracle of the car and share the needs for the journey. Karl showed no surprise as Andrew drove up to his little house.

"We knew God would provide the car for you," he explained. "And now we know you have another need."

Andrew was overwhelmed. He had not mentioned any of his financial needs to Karl. But he had learned that Karl and his prayer group were in tune with God's leading in a way that Andrew had never seen before.

"God told us you will be needing a certain amount of money for the journey you are about to go on," Karl said. "Here it is."

Karl handed Andrew an envelope. With tears of gratitude in his eyes, Andrew took the envelope from Karl. He didn't even open it to check the amount. He knew it was from God, so it would be just exactly what he needed.

With his car full of Bibles and booklets, his hands full of gifts for the journey, and his heart full of hopes and dreams, Andrew bid his family and friends goodbye and drove toward the border of Yugoslavia. As he neared the border, Andrew felt apprehension rise from deep within him. He had traveled to Communist countries before, but always as part of an official group. To maintain a welcoming appearance, the government rarely interfered with the actions of groups. But individual travelers were a different story. To break the law as an individual could mean interrogation, jail time, and even death.

The law in Yugoslavia in 1957 prohibited foreigners from bringing anything other than personal items into the country. Printed materials, in particular, were considered propaganda and were strictly forbidden. Border stations were set up at every crossing to confiscate all contraband. Andrew's car was stuffed with Bibles and portions of Bibles, considered propaganda of the worst type by the Yugoslavian government. As he approached the border station that separated him from the work God had called him to do, Andrew found himself praying.

"God," he prayed aloud into the stillness of his car, "you have called me to take your message to those who have never heard. I need your help to do this. When you were on earth, you made blind men see. Today, I pray that you will make seeing eyes blind. Blind the guards to anything you don't want them to see, Lord, and bring your Word safely to your children."

With a smile on his face and a pounding heart full of faith, Andrew drove up to the border station. He was the only car at the station, and two bored-looking guards approached him with apparent pleasure. They greeted Andrew and assured him they would just need to examine his paperwork and check through his vehicle and he would be on his way. Andrew nodded and tried to look more relaxed than he felt.

While one guard looked over Andrew's passport and visa documents, the other began poking around in the camping gear Andrew had stowed in the trunk. Andrew held his breath. Tucked into the hidden nooks of his tent and sleeping bag were Bible tracts. Suddenly the guard looked up.

"Do you have anything to declare?" he asked.

Andrew started to list his personal belongings to the guard, mentioning his watch and his camera, as well as his clothing and other personal items. The second guard was done with Andrew's documents and had begun to look inside the car as well.

"Take out that suitcase," he said, pointing. "Open it up for me."

Andrew felt sick. Bible booklets were scattered throughout the suitcase. He obediently placed it on the ground and opened it wide. The guard rummaged through the suitcase, pulling the top layer of shirts out and setting them aside. In plain view, on top of the suitcase, were two large stacks of tracts in two different Yugoslavian languages. Andrew gulped.

"It's rather dry for this time of year," Andrew said to the first guard as casually as he could. "Where I'm from, we generally have a lot more rain than this."

Andrew launched into a full discussion of life on the wet and soggy polders. The first guard listened with rapt attention, and when Andrew dared to glance at the guard who had been rummaging though the suitcase, he noticed that guard was listening too. The suitcase lay untouched, with the tracts still on top, as the guard gave his full attention to Andrew's description of life in Holland.

When Andrew caught him listening, the second guard quickly stood up. "Well, is there anything else you need to declare?" he asked.

"Just small things I carried with me," Andrew said, moving to put the shirts back into the suitcase and cover up the forbidden tracts.

"Never mind about the small things," the guard said with a smile. "Go ahead and pack things back up. Enjoy your time in Yugoslavia!"

Andrew hurried to place the suitcase back into the car. He took his passport back from the guard and thanked them. Then he drove away, praising God for His goodness and protection.

Andrew began his Yugoslavian visit in the city of Zagreb. The Dutch Bible Society had given him the name of Jamil, who was once a Bible seller in the city but had not been heard from in twelve years. Before he left Holland, Andrew sent a letter to Jamil's old address explaining the trip to Yugoslavia at the end of March and indicating Andrew would like to meet Jamil. He chose his words with caution. It was important to ensure

Jamil's safety, just in case the letter was intercepted. However, he did not know if the letter would ever reach Jamil, but he hoped that God would work a miracle and lead them to each other.

Andrew was completely unaware that the address to which he sent the letter was not where Jamil lived, and the current occupants did not know Jamil's forwarding address, so they sent the letter back to the post office. A search for Jamil ensued, and the letter was miraculously delivered to Jamil at his new address on the very day that Andrew drove into Zagreb. Jamil did not know how to get in touch with Andrew, but he felt God urging him to visit his old apartment building, where the letter was originally addressed. As Jamil walked up the sidewalk toward the old apartment building, a bright blue Volkswagen with Dutch license plates pulled up to the curb. Jamil stared in surprise.

"Are you Andrew?" Jamil asked as Andrew stepped out of the car.

"Yes," Andrew answered hesitantly.

"I am Jamil," the man said with a wide grin, shaking Andrew's hand enthusiastically. "You will not believe what God has done to bring us together today!"

Jamil and Andrew spent hours at Jamil's new home sharing stories and planning ways for Andrew to "bring greetings" to the Yugoslavian people. Jamil was happy to help Andrew set up contacts throughout the country so that as many believers as possible could be blessed by Andrew's presence. A few days later, Andrew and his interpreter—a young engineering student named Nikola—headed into the Yugoslavian countryside in the little blue car.

Over the course of his seven weeks in Yugoslavia, Andrew held more than eighty meetings, often speaking up to a half-dozen times each Sunday, and holding smaller meetings during the week. Other than having to register with the police in each new district he entered, Andrew was surprised at the level of freedom he experienced. But as he became more familiar with the country and the people, Andrew began to see the tactics being used by the government to wear down the believers. They were keeping the young people from forming attachments to the church. In doing so, they were waiting for the church to die off with the older generations.

In one village, Andrew met a little girl named Marta, playing by the street in the middle of the day. He asked Nikola why she was not in school. Nikola questioned Marta's mother.

"Before Marta started school," her mother said, "she was accustomed to saying a prayer before her meals. So when it came time for lunch at school, Marta prayed out loud, just as she always did at home."

"What happened?" Andrew asked.

Marta's mother sighed. "The teacher was angry. She shouted at Marta and told her she was wicked and was filling the other children's heads with nonsense. The teacher told Marta she must never pray again. And when Marta prayed—out of habit—before lunch the next day, she was expelled and forbidden to attend school again."

Stories like this were commonplace throughout the country, but in the region of Macedonia, the fear and persecution rose to a new level. It was the poorest province of the country, and the area in which Communism had its strongest hold, forcing believers to worship God creatively. One Sunday morning Andrew and Nikola had a meeting scheduled at a small Macedonian church at 10:00. When they arrived, they found the church building empty. They waited patiently until 11:00, but no one came. As Andrew reached his car to leave, a villager strolled up to him.

"Are you the visiting pastor from Holland?" the man asked.

"I am," Andrew answered.

The man smiled and shook Andrew's hand vigorously. "Thank you so much for being with us today," he said warmly. "May God be with you on your journey."

With that, he walked away. Andrew and Nikola exchanged puzzled glances. Just as they were about to get into the car, another villager strolled up. He also asked Andrew if he was the visiting pastor. Like the previous man, this man thanked Andrew and wished him well. Now Andrew was smiling, and as he glanced over, he saw Nikola smiling too. This was a new way to have church! Over the next forty-five minutes, nearly every person in the village passed by Andrew's car and repeated the scene, brilliantly demonstrating the power of faith over fear.

A few days later, Andrew was scheduled to speak at an evening service in another Macedonian town. The pastor hosted Andrew and Nikola for dinner at his house before the eight o'clock service. At 7:55, Andrew suggested they head for the nearby church.

"No," said the pastor. "It is not time yet."

At 8:15, Andrew spoke up again. "Don't you think we ought to head for the church now? I'm sure people will be waiting."

The pastor rose from his seat and crossed to the window. He peered out and shook his head.

"No," he said again. "It is still not time yet."

At 8:30, the pastor glanced out the window again and smiled. "Now it is time," he said. "You see, the people will not come to church until after dark. It isn't illegal to come to church, but here we need to be careful."

As the pastor walked Andrew and Nikola the short distance to the church, Andrew noticed flickering lanterns bobbing through the fields toward the little church building. People came in groups of two or three, their faces bent low. Once inside the church, the need for secrecy was forgotten, and the lamps were hung high to give the sanctuary a warm glow. More than two hundred people came through the night to hear Andrew speak, and eighty-five of them committed their lives to Christ before leaving.

After several weeks in Yugoslavia, Andrew and Nikola arrived in Belgrade. The services on Sunday surprised Andrew. Much of his Yugoslavian ministry had been in small country churches with simple, uneducated peasants who welcomed him with open arms and open hearts. But Belgrade was the big city, with a sophisticated, wealthy, educated metropolitan crowd. Andrew expected a much more humble showing and a much less enthusiastic response.

To his surprise, he found the church packed to capacity that morning, with well-dressed families wedged into pews elbow-to-elbow and standing along the sides of the building. They crowded against the narrow platform, and halfway through the service, Andrew watched a group of men take a door off its hinges so the overflow crowd could hear more clearly.

At the end of the service, Andrew and Nikola gave an altar call. They asked anyone who wanted to commit their life to Christ or reaffirm a previous commitment to raise their hand. Every hand in the building went up. Afraid they had not understood the seriousness of this commitment in the face of potential persecution, Andrew explained the concept again. This time, he asked those who were interested in making this life-changing commitment to stand. Not one person in the whole building remained seated. They all got to their feet.

Andrew began to encourage the believers—old and new—to pray daily and spend time in God's Word.

"Brother Andrew, what you have said about prayer is powerful. We will do this. We can pray every day," the pastor said sadly. He paused and gave an embarrassed little cough. "But what you said about Bible reading is impossible. You see, most of these people do not have Bibles."

Andrew was stunned. He expected such situations in the isolated country churches, but not in the big city, not in Belgrade.

"How many of you have Bibles?" Andrew asked the congregation.

Seven hands went up. Andrew felt desperate. He had no more Bibles to distribute, and the people were so hungry for the Word of God. After the service, Andrew, Nikola, and the pastor sat down and worked out a Bible-sharing schedule, comprised of a combination of group study and individual use, with a certain number of hours allotted to each member per day.

It was a workable solution, but not a good one. Andrew left Belgrade feeling overwhelmingly burdened to do more. He promised God he would continue his work until Bibles rested in every hand that desired them. He vowed to find ways to slip through the Iron Curtain over and over again, bringing the light of God's Word into the darkness. And as he crossed the border on his way out of Yugoslavia, Andrew knew the adventure was only just beginning.

On the Threshold of
the Future

As Andrew rolled across Europe in his little blue Volkswagen, he found himself wrestling with questions. How could he get Bibles into nations where printed material was forbidden? How could he smuggle thousands of books when many people found themselves in jail for simply carrying a handful of pamphlets? How could he disciple new converts and encourage established believers? How could he strengthen the pastors to faithfully endure in the face of such challenges?

For six weeks after he arrived back in Witte, Andrew focused his energies on telling his story. He accepted speaking engagements, wrote articles, and shared with anyone who would listen. He drove to Amsterdam and told the Whetstras what an amazing job the faithful little Volkswagen had done carrying him through the Yugoslavian countryside. He went to Amersfoort and visited Karl de Graaf and his prayer group. He kept moving and stayed busy, but he was desperately lonely.

He had asked God before to send him a wife who could share in his ministry, cry with him during the tough times, and rejoice with him in the miracles. In July 1957, Andrew asked God one more time. At first, there seemed to be no answer. Then, in September, God put someone on Andrew's heart: Corrie van Dam.

With sudden urgency, Andrew drove to Alkmaar, where he and Corrie had worked in the factory together and where her parents had lived. He drove straight to her old house, but the shutters were closed and the lawn was overgrown. Andrew went to Ringers' Chocolate Factory to see if anyone knew where the van Dam family had moved. Mr Ringers was thrilled to see Andrew, but he did not know where the van Dams were living. He did say Corrie had taken her nurse's training at St. Elizabeth's Hospital in Haarlem, and she might still be living there.

Hope surged in Andrew's heart as he headed for Haarlem. He could think of a hundred reasons to go there: speaking invitations he had received, Bible stores he needed to visit, people he wanted to see. If he was honest, however, the real reason he was headed for Haarlem was the possibility that Corrie might be there. Just outside town, he stopped at a gas station and called St. Elizabeth's Hospital. The receptionist told him Corrie was a final-year nursing student and was living in an apartment in town. She gave Andrew the address.

Andrew visited the address and learned Corrie's father was very ill, and she had traveled back to Alkmaar to help care for him. The family had moved to a small apartment to make life easier for Mr van Dam. Corrie's landlord gave Andrew the address of the apartment. After finishing his business and fulfilling his obligations in Haarlem, Andrew headed eagerly back to Alkmaar.

When Andrew knocked on the apartment door, Corrie answered it. She was all grown up and prettier than he remembered.

"I heard that your father is ill, and I have come to visit him," Andrew said, half truthfully.

Corrie smiled and led Andrew to her father's room. For over an hour, Andrew shared his stories with Mr van Dam, who was thrilled to have a visitor. Corrie came and went as they talked, and Andrew tried not to stare at her. Somehow it was enough just to be near her.

Andrew began visiting twice a week, spending most of his time with Mr van Dam, but reveling in the few minutes of private conversation he had with Corrie as he arrived and left each time. He was certain Corrie was the girl for him, but every time he tried to imagine himself proposing to her, he felt like a fool. What could he offer someone so wonderful? He had no material goods, no stability in his life, no guarantee that he would not end up imprisoned behind the Iron Curtain. He felt asking her to share his crazy life was unreasonable and unfair.

In the midst of his visits to Mr van Dam, a letter arrived from the Hungarian consulate granting Andrew a visa. As he stared at the visa, Andrew knew it was the perfect opportunity to propose to Corrie. He would ask her to marry him immediately, but wouldn't accept her answer until he returned from Hungary. That would give her an idea of what life with him would be like—infrequent contact and a wealth of wondering and worrying for weeks on end. At the end of his trip, he was sure her answer would reflect God's will for his life.

Andrew was so excited about his plan that he jumped in the car and drove straight to Alkmaar. He rushed up to the apartment door, excitement and joy dancing across his face. But when Corrie answered his enthusiastic knock, Andrew's heart deflated. Her face was red and swollen from crying, and her eyes told him all he needed to know. Her father was gone.

The timing was wrong, so Andrew tried to be patient. He saw Corrie at the funeral, but otherwise he chose to give her time and space to grieve and be with her family. For three weeks, Andrew feverishly gathered every Hungarian Bible and tract he could find. He hid them in every nook and cranny of his car, planning carefully and rearranging regularly. If his materials were confiscated, they would serve no purpose to the Hungarian believers.

When he could wait no longer, Andrew drove to Corrie's house and invited her to go for a drive. They parked overlooking a moonlit canal, and they gazed out over the glistening water in pleasant silence. Finally, Andrew spoke.

"Corrie," he said, "I love you. I want you to marry me. But here's the thing—I have nothing to offer you. And my life is a hard life. It would probably be even harder for you."

He tried to explain what his life was like, how often he would be gone, and how lonely she might be. He stressed the uncertainties and infrequent contact. And then he told her to think about it until he returned from Hungary, giving her a few months of experience with the life he lived.

"Oh, Corrie," Andrew pleaded miserably, "you'd be crazy to marry a guy like me, but I really do hope you'll say yes!"

Days later, Andrew left for Hungary with the promise of Corrie's answer when he returned. As he drove, he felt lonelier than ever. Now that he had someone to leave behind, he found it harder to go. Finally he found himself safely across the border. He rolled into the Hungarian countryside with every Bible and tract still stashed securely in his car.

Feeling unusually confident and terribly hungry, Andrew turned off the main road and down a well-worn lane near the Danube River. He unloaded a few boxes full of tracts and pulled out his picnic supplies. He had just begun cooking his lunch when the whine of an engine caught his attention. A speedboat sliced through the water, headed straight for him. As the boat drew nearer, Andrew could see a soldier standing in the bow with a gun pointed straight at him. Andrew's stomach knotted up and his breath came in quick, shallow bursts. Silently, he prayed for protection and peace.

When the boat pulled up along the shore, the soldier with the gun stayed in place while the other two soldiers hopped out and headed straight for Andrew's car. Refusing to turn around, Andrew continued to cook his lunch, and he began speaking in Dutch, taking out extra plates and motioning for the soldiers to join him. The soldiers glared at Andrew and shook their heads as they rummaged through his car. When the food was ready, Andrew decided to eat.

As he filled his plate, he hesitated, wondering if he should pray over his food. Christians were especially hated in Hungary because of their role in the Hungarian Revolt. But to allow fear to keep him from praying seemed more dangerous to Andrew than anything the soldiers could do to him. With a deep breath and God-given determination, Andrew folded his hands, bowed his head, and began to pray in Dutch.

While he was praying, the rummaging noises stopped. As he ended his prayer, Andrew heard his car door slam shut. The soldiers turned abruptly, hurried to their boat, and sped away down the river. Andrew quickly packed up his belongings and, with a sigh of relief, headed back down the road.

As he made his way into Budapest, Andrew was struck by the contrasting beauty of the ancient city and scars from the Hungarian Revolt. Andrew drove through the streets, praying over the city and praying for God's guidance. Address in hand, Andrew found Professor B, a well-known teacher at an elite school and a faithful believer in God. Over the years, Professor B had managed to carefully juggle his personal beliefs with his public persona to maintain his position. But with Andrew's arrival, all that was about to change.

"I would like you to be my interpreter while I am in Hungary," Andrew told Professor B. "I realize this could cost you everything, so I will understand if you cannot do this for me."

Professor B put a hand on Andrew's shoulder. "Of course I will be your interpreter," he said. "In the end, I will lose everything anyway. I would rather lose it for the cause of Christ than for any other pursuit."

The two men shook hands and became brothers-in-arms in the war against darkness. With a sly grin, Andrew led Professor B to his car, parked out on the street. He glanced around and, after making sure they weren't being watched, pulled away one of the secret panels on the car. When Professor B saw the stacks of Bibles hidden inside, his eyes widened.

"How many did you manage to bring?" he asked.

"There are many hidden compartments," Andrew said. "Each one is packed full."

"It is a miracle," Professor B whispered. "There are many churches open and operating without a single Bible available to them. You will be very busy here, speaking and distributing Bibles. But you must remember there will also be some risk involved."

Professor B explained that the government was wary of all Christians. Many pastors had spent time in prison. Churches were under constant scrutiny, and those that were perceived to be in opposition to the Communist government were persecuted and shut down.

"Many churches compromise their beliefs," Professor B admitted sadly. "But some refuse, and those churches pay a high price."

Andrew remembered the church he had first visited in Poland, where the pastor indicated that compromise was inevitable. It seemed to be a sentiment that crossed borders in these Communist nations. Churches accepted Communist beliefs so they could stay open and operating, but in doing so, they rejected the Spirit of God and became mere social clubs. True gospel messages were rare and risky.

Andrew was discouraged by the culture of compromise, but Professor B encouraged him with a new take on evangelism.

"I want you to conduct a wedding this afternoon," Professor B told Andrew.

"A wedding?" Andrew was perplexed. "That isn't usually something I do."

Professor B grinned. "This will be a wedding like none you've ever been to before. When your turn comes, I want you to say a few sentences of congratulations to the bride and groom. Then I want you to preach the strongest salvation message that they have ever heard!"

"At a wedding?" Andrew asked.

"People are afraid to come into church except for weddings and funerals," Professor B explained. "And for the most part, the government does not dare interfere with these two events. So when a wedding or funeral comes along, we use it as a tool to evangelize everyone who attends."

Andrew smiled. It reminded him of the tradition of "bringing greetings" that he had experienced in Czechoslovakia and Yugoslavia. When the wedding was over, Andrew introduced Professor B to the concept of "bringing greetings." As Andrew spoke, excitement spread across the professor's face.

"Let's do it," he nearly shouted. "I'll make some calls."

That night, Andrew and Professor B held their first meeting at a large church in Budapest. The next night, they held a similar meeting in a different church. Each night, at the end of the service, they announced the time and place for the next meeting. People began queueing by mid-afternoon to hear Andrew speak.

"We are attracting too much attention," Professor B worried. "We need a new tactic."

They stopped announcing the time and place of the next meeting and simply said there would be a meeting. On the afternoon of the meeting, a calling system was used to inform people of the location and time. Andrew never got tired of seeing the pews fill with people who were hungry to hear the Word of God.

Each night, Andrew noticed Professor B and the church pastors were looking over the assembly, studying each face. When he asked the professor about it, Professor B said they were watching for secret police. The professor and the pastors were anxious about the threat of a visit from the secret police, and Andrew began to feel nervous, too.

"They're here," Professor B warned Andrew one night as he looked out into the crowded room. "Come with me."

They slipped off the platform and into the pastor's office, where two policemen were waiting for them. They questioned Andrew and Professor B extensively. Then they handed them a summons to appear in court the next day.

At 9:00 the next morning, Andrew and Professor B walked into police headquarters. Because of his position at the school, Professor B knew most of the personnel at police headquarters.

"We would be much better off if we were seeing the deputy," he said. "Unfortunately, we are scheduled to appear before the head of the department."

They were ushered into a room to wait. An hour passed. Then two. After almost three hours of waiting, just before noon, a clerk appeared and led them down a long hallway. They stopped in front of the deputy's office.

"You were scheduled to appear before the department head," the clerk explained. "But late last night he became very ill. You will have to appear before the deputy instead."

Andrew and Professor B exchanged hopeful glances. Twenty minutes later, they left the building as free men, with only a warning against their disruptive behavior. As usual, God had worked out the details.

Because future meetings in Budapest were not possible, Professor B arranged for Andrew to spend his last few weeks in Hungary in the eastern part of the country. To prevent further police problems, Professor B sent a different interpreter with Andrew. The tour went well, and people flocked to hear Andrew, who had become quite famous by word of mouth.

When he returned to Budapest before leaving the country, Andrew visited Professor B and his son, Janos, a prominent young attorney. He was surprised to find them both at home in the middle of the day, but they seemed so cheerful, he didn't worry about it. They thanked him for coming and for allowing them to be a part of his mission. Then they bid him farewell and prayed God's blessings over all that he did.

Later, Andrew received a letter from Professor B, hand-carried out of Hungary by a friend. In it, the professor explained that both he and Janos had been forced to resign their positions. They had lost all their earthly possessions, but their hearts were full of gratitude.

"Many have given more for the cause of Christ," the professor wrote. "Do not be sad for us, brother. We are praising the Lord that we are counted worthy to suffer for Him."

A New Wife and a New Life

As the little blue Volkswagen rolled toward Holland, Andrew felt growing anticipation. He wondered if Corrie would say yes to his proposal. When he crossed the border, he could not wait any longer. He bypassed Witte and drove straight to St. Elizabeth's Hospital in Haarlem. Corrie was just finishing up a long shift, but when she saw Andrew, the tired lines disappeared from her face.

"Oh, Corrie," Andrew said, "I want you to know that I love you, whether you say yes or no."

Corrie's laughter sounded like bells in Andrew's heart. "I love you too, Andrew," she admitted. "And I want to be your wife!"

The next week, Andrew and Corrie picked out wedding rings together at a jeweler in Haarlem. That night, as they sat together in Corrie's apartment, Andrew took her hand.

"I don't know where the road will lead us," he admitted.

"Well," Corrie said, "wherever the road may lead, we will walk it together."

Andrew and Corrie were married June 27th, 1958 in Alkmaar, surrounded by friends and family and fond memories. The whole crew from Ringers' Chocolate Factory was there, along with Uncle Hoppy from London and a band of friends from WEC headquarters. There was also a busload of nurses from the hospital and a handful of workers from the refugee camps. Corrie's family and Andrew's family were there, as well as friends from Witte and the Whetstras from Amsterdam. It was a day filled with joy and laughter, a beautiful beginning to Andrew and Corrie's life together.

After their honeymoon, Corrie and Andrew moved into the little room above the shed in Witte. It had been so lonely and empty for Andrew alone, but with Corrie there, it suddenly seemed full of sunshine and promise. But soon it became literally full of bundles of clothing and goods for the refugees in the camps. Andrew had been so successful in his talks across Holland that donations were pouring in. In the first year of speaking engagements, more than eight tons of donations were sent to the tiny house in Witte.

The only place to store the abundant donations was in Andrew and Corrie's room. The clothing that came in was mostly unwashed, bringing fleas and other unwelcome visitors into the room. Each time Andrew made a trip to the camps, he packed the little Volkswagen until he could barely squeeze into the driver's seat, but donations came in faster than he could carry them out.

Finally, as fall drew near, Andrew decided Corrie should see the camps for herself. So they packed up the back seat of the car and headed out to the camps of West Berlin. Corrie was eager to use her nursing skills to help the hopeless people there, and Andrew was eager to have his beloved wife beside him in his ministry.

As Andrew and Corrie began working together among the refugees, Andrew began to see more about life behind the Iron Curtain. Closer to the countries of the West, Communist nations like Poland, Czechoslovakia, Yugoslavia, East Germany, and Hungary were lighter-handed in their persecution of those who did not conform to the standards of the State. Deep within the heart of Communism, however, were countries like Rumania, Bulgaria, Albania, and Russia, places where defying the State often meant death. These were the nations Andrew ultimately felt led to reach with God's Word.

There was only one country near the West that Andrew had not yet visited: East Germany. Because he was already in West Germany working in the camps, Andrew felt he was in the perfect position to travel there. He decided to discuss his thoughts with Corrie.

"I think we need to go to East Germany," Andrew said to Corrie as they prepared for bed one night.

"Oh, Andy," she said, "I couldn't possibly leave the camps now. There is so much left to do!"

Andrew studied her carefully. There were bags under her eyes and she was paler than before, but she was bright with ambition. Since they had come to the camps, she had worked at a feverish pace, setting up classes and clinics, improving hygiene, healing wounded bodies, and touching wounded souls. He wondered if he had been wrong to plunge Corrie into life in the camps. He wondered if she had been ready to deal with such sadness.

Propelled by a desire to pull Corrie away from the darkness of the camps Andrew applied for two visas to East Germany. Within days, the visas were granted. Andrew brought them joyfully to Corrie.

"You go, Andy," she said, her arms spread wide. "This is where I belong. I wouldn't be any good there anyway. I don't speak German and I can't preach. But I can help here."

When Andrew protested, Corrie took both his hands in hers. "Andrew, we knew this life would bring times of separation," she reminded him. "You go where you're needed, and I'll stay where I'm needed. And we will both have stories to tell when you return."

When Andrew crossed into East Germany at a checkpoint in the Berlin Wall, he could feel the oppression. People hurried silently through the streets. No one laughed. No one smiled. No one spoke. There was a sadness and fear that hung over everything. Police lingered in doorways and lurked on street corners. They randomly stopped civilians, tearing briefcases apart and pillaging handbags with no explanation or excuse. No one protested. The people simply cowered in fear.

A handful of refugees had given Andrew the name of a pastor in the southern part of East Germany. His name was Wilhelm, and he and his wife, Mar, were youth workers in a church up in the hills. Andrew pulled up to Wilhelm's house on a sunny afternoon and parked next to a rickety old motorbike. Wilhelm and Mar immediately invited Andrew inside for a cup of coffee.

"We are so glad you have come," Wilhelm said. He paused as a deep cough racked his body. "Our journey can be discouraging at times. What a blessing it is that you have come to encourage us!"

"Do you need Bibles?" Andrew asked eagerly.

"Oh, no," Wilhelm said, leading Andrew to his little office and pointing to a stack of Bibles. "We have plenty of Bibles. And we have seminaries that actually train people in the Word of God. We also hold large rallies and evangelistic meetings without any interference or persecution."

Andrew was confused. "But I thought you needed encouragement."

"We do," Wilhelm insisted, his fists clenching and unclenching. "The government is trying a new tactic. They have learned that direct attacks only strengthen the church. But indirect attacks are highly effective. Luring people away in the name of patriotism keeps them out of the church." He paused to cough again, doubling over in an effort to catch his breath. "Come with me to the service this afternoon. You will see what I mean."

Andrew suggested Wilhelm could ride in his car, and Mar smiled.

"Thank you," she said. "It's all those trips on that motorbike that make him cough so much."

Wilhelm shook his head and kissed his wife. "She worries too much," he said to Andrew. "Let's get going."

They traveled through the hills to a nearby town for a meeting of pastors. Most of the pastors got up and read statistics from their districts. Wilhelm quietly explained the statistics to Andrew. The State had developed services to mirror the services of the church, and the statistics represented church participation in these ceremonies. Once Andrew understood the meaning of the statistics, he listened with growing uneasiness. Up to 70% of church members were choosing to participate in State ceremonies over the traditional church meetings. Churches simply could not compete with the pressures of friends, neighbors, colleagues, and classmates.

"This is why we need encouragement," Wilhelm explained. "We could resist an up-front attack. But these subtle and successful attempts to draw people away have caused the church to turn in and become isolated. God has sent you to remind us that we are not alone, and we can be conquerors through His power."

For two weeks, Andrew travelled with Wilhelm throughout the southern districts of East Germany.

He saw dozens of churches that had plenty of Bibles but few dedicated believers. He encouraged them to think of themselves as missionaries, and to think of their nation as a mission field. Over and over, Andrew preached this message to pastors and people who had lost the will to fight.

After the service in one town, a man stood up and said, "Brother Andrew, it is easy for you to talk about missionary work. You are free to travel throughout Europe. You can be a missionary. But I cannot even travel outside my own country. How can I be a missionary?"

Andrew reminded the man that his country was filled with occupying Russian soldiers and with East Germans who did not believe.

"Don't complain that you can't go to the mission field," Andrew chided. "Praise God that He has brought the mission field to you!"

When Andrew left East Germany, he searched the camps of West Berlin, looking for Corrie. He found her inspecting children for lice in the dirtiest part of an overcrowded camp. Seeing her was both a blessing and a shock. She was thinner, paler, with a yellowish tinge to her skin. There were dark circles under her eyes, but she smiled brightly when she saw Andrew.

"Welcome home," she said softly.

Andrew knew he needed to get her out of the camps and away from the horrors for a while. He took her passport and his passport and went to the Yugoslavian consulate. His friends in Yugoslavia desperately needed

Bibles, and the countryside was calm and beautiful, just what Corrie needed to wipe the sadness from her eyes. The visas were granted immediately, and Andrew spent the rest of the day buying up Bibles and planning their trip.

Although Corrie protested, Andrew was determined. Finally, she agreed to travel with him, and they set out on their first trip behind the Iron Curtain together. Assuming they were newlyweds, the border guards barely glanced at their overstuffed luggage. Instead, they offered advice on tourist destinations. It was the easiest crossing Andrew had ever experienced.

In Belgrade, Andrew and Corrie met with Jamil and Nikola, Andrew's friends from his first trip. They took him around to visit all the churches, distributing Bibles to wide-eyed believers along the way. The men thumped Andrew on the back, the women kissed Corrie, and everyone cried tears of joy. It was a time of great celebration.

For six days, Andrew preached and they all ministered. But during dinner on the seventh day, the police descended swiftly on the house where they were eating. Corrie, whose health was not improving, was in a bedroom resting while the rest of the team sat around a low table talking and laughing over a meal. There was a sudden knock on the door and two uniformed policemen burst into the room.

"Come with us!" they ordered Andrew.

"Where?"

"No talking," they barked. "You will come with us!"

Corrie came to the doorway, pale and shaken. "What's going on?" she asked.

"Is she with you?" the officers asked.

Andrew nodded, moving to stand beside Corrie, who was swaying slightly.

"Then she must come too," the officers ordered.

Andrew and Corrie were taken to police headquarters. They were told they would have to leave the country immediately. Their visas were being revoked because of their illegal activities. At police headquarters, Andrew and Corrie's passports were marked with a large red stamp indicating they were no longer permitted to enter Yugoslavia. Then they were escorted to the border.

As they drove through the darkness toward Holland and home, Andrew wanted to be angry. He wanted to understand God's purpose in revoking their visas. But all he could do was glance over at Corrie, feebly dozing in the passenger seat. Already physically ill, she was emotionally shaken by their arrest and removal from Yugoslavia. On the trip home, Andrew had to frequently stop the car so Corrie could vomit and then lie on the cool roadside grass until her nausea passed. All Andrew could think of was getting Corrie home where a doctor could examine her. He couldn't shake the thought that something was seriously wrong.

Persisting through the Problems

Back at the little house in Witte, Andrew got Corrie settled into bed. Then he called the doctor and described her symptoms. The doctor came at once. He spent a long time with Corrie in the little room while Andrew waited outside. Finally, the doctor came out, smiling and packing his little black bag.

"Will she be okay?" Andrew asked, tension in his voice.

"Your wife will be fine, Andrew," the doctor said. "I gave her some pills for the nausea and told her to visit me in a month."

"But what is the diagnosis?" Andrew pressed, still filled with concern.

The doctor studied Andrew's anxious face carefully. "You really don't have any idea, do you?" the doctor said with a chuckle. "Congratulations, Andrew! You're going to be a father."

Andrew pushed past the doctor and dashed up the ladder to the little room. Corrie was in bed, grinning widely. Andrew let out a delighted whoop. She was going to have a baby!

Just after they returned to Holland, two letters came through offering Andrew visas to Bulgaria and Rumania, two of the most difficult countries to enter. Andrew was overjoyed, but apprehensive. It seemed God was opening the door to the deepest, darkest strongholds of Communism, and Andrew was eager to walk right in. But now he had a wife and a child on the way. He had to think about what would happen if he was captured or killed.

He also had that ugly red stamp from Yugoslavia in his passport. He couldn't tear out the page, and pretending he had lost his passport seemed somehow dishonest. A quick trip to a government office, however, yielded a valuable tip from a helpful clerk. Andrew started making day trips to nearby countries and insisting they stamp his passport. Within a few weeks, his passport was full, and he had a true need to apply for a new one. Now, if only he could bring himself to leave Corrie.

They cried together, talked together, prayed together, and eventually stashed the Rumanian and Bulgarian Bibles in the little blue Volkswagen together. On the morning Andrew was scheduled to leave, they were both reluctant to say goodbye.

"Do you have the clothes for the refugees? Money? And your tent and cooking supplies?" Corrie worried.

"I have everything this little car can possibly hold," Andrew assured her.

"Please come back to us, Andrew," Corrie said, tears in her eyes. "This baby and I need you."

As the miles flew beneath the wheels of his vehicle, Andrew thought about the money in his wallet. Several unexpected donations had come in, and Andrew had tried to leave the excess money with Corrie, but she insisted he take it with him. He knew it had to be from God, and he wondered what he might need it for.

Andrew felt a twinge of nervousness as he neared the Yugoslavian border. It had only been a few months since he had been expelled from Yugoslavia, but that was the only logical route to Bulgaria. Every other route would take Andrew more than a thousand miles out of his way and would cost him several days of travel time. He had applied for another Yugoslavian visa, and it had been granted, due largely to the disorganized Yugoslavian paperwork system. Still, he hated to count on inefficiency for his safety.

Andrew whispered a prayer as he approached the border station. The guard looked over his paperwork and chatted with him, and then waved him through. Andrew breathed a sigh of relief. He figured he had about four days of leeway before his border crossing papers went to Belgrade and they realized he was in the country. Andrew hoped to be long gone by then.

By the end of the fourth day in Yugoslavia, Andrew was near the border and had experienced no problems from the authorities. He decided to stay one more day. On the evening of the fifth day, he checked into a hotel. He gave the desk clerk his passport and settled into a room for some much-needed rest.

Just before dawn, two government officials knocked on Andrew's door. They ordered him to dress and follow them. Still shaking the cobwebs of sleep from his brain, Andrew slipped into pants and a shirt and followed the men into a nearby building. At the end of a long corridor, he entered a tidy office where a man with a craggy face sat behind a wide metal desk.

"Andrew van der Bijl, why did you come back to Yugoslavia?" the man asked. Without waiting for a response, he continued. "You will leave immediately. You will not speak with anyone else in Yugoslavia. You will leave through the border crossing at Trieste within twenty-four hours."

With that, the man lifted the familiar red stamp and marked Andrew's passport in three places, marring three different pages. Andrew felt panic rise in his soul. Trieste was in the northwest corner of Yugoslavia, back toward Holland and far away from Bulgaria. He tried to reason with the grumpy man behind the desk.

"Please, sir," Andrew begged, as respectfully as possible, "I'm headed to Bulgaria. Couldn't I leave by a border crossing closer to my destination?"

"I said Trieste," the man snapped. And with that, the interview was over.

As he drove toward Trieste, Andrew began to understand why so much extra money had come in for his journey. Taking the round-trip route through Italy and Greece would be 1500 miles out of his way, but he had no choice. A cloud of doubt, depression, and despair settled heavily over his soul. Had the presence and blessing of God left his ministry?

The journey was slow and the roads were rough, dotted with potholes and washouts. Donkeys and horse-drawn carts competed with cars for precedence in the narrow lanes. Many days, Andrew did little more than inch along. He missed Corrie's birthday as he traveled down the coast of Italy. He worried about the new red stamps in his passport. He wondered if he would be home for the birth of his baby. And then his back began to act up, the nagging aftereffect of a slipped disk he had suffered a few years earlier. The pain took Andrew's frustration to a new level.

One morning, Andrew was bumping along the rutted roads when he saw a small blue sign. Above the indecipherable Greek letters was a single word in Latin: Filippi. Andrew slammed on the brakes and pulled over. He climbed carefully out of the car, wincing at the shooting pain in his back. Just off the road, behind a chain-link fence, were the crumbling ruins of an ancient city. This was Philippi, the city from the Bible where Paul and Silas were singing in prison. This was the city where God sent an angel and an earthquake to free His servants from their darkness and despair.

In that moment, Andrew could almost hear the voice of God echoing through the centuries, saying, "Where is your faith? I have never left you, never forsaken you." With sudden shock, Andrew realized the pain in his back was gone. Indescribable joy flooded his spirit. God had brought him on a mammoth detour to remind him there was no hole so deep, no prison so dark that God was not with Andrew, beside him every step of the way. Filled with a new assurance of God's goodness, Andrew bumped his way across Turkey, ready to tackle his biggest obstacle yet: the border of Bulgaria.

Beginnings in Bulgaria

Compared with other border experiences Andrew had faced, crossing the border into Bulgaria was a dream. The border guard barely glanced into his car. He did not ask Andrew to open any suitcases or remove any items. Instead, he gave a carefully practiced speech in English, welcoming Andrew to Bulgaria. As he drove away from the border, Andrew grinned, feeling foolish for spending so much time worrying about the Bulgarian border crossing.

The main roads throughout the countryside were wide and well paved. Children ran alongside the car as Andrew passed through sleepy little villages. Men and women waved and smiled. Everything seemed remarkably picturesque.

On his last night in Yugoslavia, a man in one of the churches had asked Andrew to contact his best friend, a man named Petroff who lived in Sofia, Bulgaria. The man told Andrew that Petroff was a faithful saint and would be thrilled to help Andrew. Andrew had memorized Petroff's address, and he headed to Sofia, anxious to see how God would help him to do this work in another Communist country.

Sofia was a large city, so Andrew hoped to find a map at the hotel when he checked in. He planned to study the map to find his way to Petroff's address.

"Do you have a map I could borrow?" Andrew asked the hotel desk clerk as he checked in and received his room keys.

The clerk shook his head. "All I have is this tiny, hand-painted map. It may not be very helpful though, as it only has the largest streets marked."

Andrew bent over the little map, flattened beneath the countertop glass. The clerk was right. Only the main streets were featured on the map, and Petroff's address was in a residential neighborhood, not on a main road. But one tiny side street was marked on the map, out of place among the large boulevards. And that one small side street the mapmaker had included was Petroff's street. Andrew tried to suppress his grin as he thanked the clerk and headed to his room.

The next day, Andrew made his way through the early morning sunshine to Petroff's street. As Andrew reached Petroff's large apartment building, a man from the opposite direction also turned in at the walkway. Andrew glanced at the other man and felt a surge of recognition pulse through his body. He had never met the man before, but somehow he knew it was Petroff. For a mere instant, their eyes met, and Andrew saw recognition flash in the man's eyes as well.

Trusting this was a meeting orchestrated by God, Andrew followed the man into the building and up the stairs. Neither spoke, but each seemed to understand the spiritual connection they had. On the far side of the building, the man took out a key and opened the door to a tiny, one-room apartment. Andrew walked through the door in faith, and the man closed the door behind them, not bothering to turn on a light.

"My name is Andrew," he spoke into the darkness. "I have come from Holland to minister to you."

The man breathed a sigh of relief and reached for a light. "I am Petroff," he responded. "Welcome to Bulgaria."

From a corner of the shadowy room, Petroff's wife came forward. All three joined hands and dropped to their knees, thanking God for bringing them together in such a miraculous way. They praised God that no risk was required, and that they had been led directly to one another. Then Andrew began to ask questions.

"I have heard there is a need for Bibles here in Bulgaria," he told Petroff. "Is this true?"

In a wordless answer, Petroff led Andrew to an old typewriter on a desk. Beside the typewriter was a Bible open to the book of Exodus. In the typewriter was a sheet of paper, and it was clear that someone had been typing the book of Exodus, word for word. On the dining table, Petroff picked up another Bible.

"Bibles are impossible to find," he admitted. "I found this one last week, but it is missing Genesis, Exodus, and Revelation. I paid a whole month's wages for this Bible. So now I just need to type the missing books from my own Bible, and it will be complete."

"What will you do with it?" Andrew asked.

"Give it away," Petroff's wife answered. "To a little church where there are no Bibles. They need it far more than we do."

"There are many churches in Bulgaria without a single Bible," Petroff said. "It is the same in Rumania and Russia. Bibles were scarce, even in the old days. But since the Communist takeover …" Petroff shook his head and spread his empty hands wide in an exaggerated shrug.

"My dear brother," Andrew said, excitement rising in his throat, "I have something wonderful to show you."

That night, under cover of darkness, Andrew drove the little blue Volkswagen down Petroff's street. He checked the street to make sure he was not being watched and carefully unloaded a heavy crate of Bibles. He carried the box up to Petroff's apartment and set it on the dining table. Petroff's eyes were wide as he and his wife watched with mounting curiosity. Andrew removed the lid and took out a Bulgarian Bible. He placed it in Petroff's shaking hands. Andrew took out another Bible and handed it to Petroff's wife.

"Are there more?" she asked, not daring to look in the box.

"This box is full," Andrew said, "and there are more boxes, just like this one, in the car outside."

Petroff's eyes were closed. He could not speak, but tears streamed down his cheeks. They dripped off his chin and splashed onto the Bible he was holding. Andrew felt tears fill his own eyes. This was why he had come to Bulgaria—to bring the blessings of the Bible to hungry people.

Petroff and Andrew immediately set out on a missionary journey through Bulgaria, taking Bibles to the underground churches that needed them most. As they travelled through the rolling green countryside, Petroff explained that there were two types of churches in Bulgaria. Many large churches operated openly, but their sermons centered on the glories of Communism and the new regime. The Word of God was secondary to the will of the State in these churches. In stark contrast underground churches operated in secret, opposing the rules and rites of Communism and maintaining the true message. If the government found out these churches were holding services, they would be shut down immediately and the participants would be thrown in jail.

A few days into their journey, Petroff took Andrew to one of these secret services. It took place in a tiny apartment on the third floor of an old apartment building. There were only twelve people in attendance, but it took more than an hour for everyone to arrive. They had to space their entry so it would not appear that anything out of the ordinary was taking place. Everything was scheduled.

Behind Enemy Lines

Everything was structured. Everything was carefully planned to prevent detection.

At 7:30, Petroff turned to Andrew. "It is our time," he said quietly. "No talking. Just follow me and do whatever I do."

Together, Andrew and Petroff approached the ancient building. They turned in together at the walk and silently climbed to the third floor. They strode quietly to the end of a long corridor. Then, without knocking or announcing their presence in any way, Petroff threw open an apartment door and pulled Andrew inside, quietly closing the door behind them. Eight eager faces welcomed them with silent smiles. They had arrived in the underground church.

As they waited for the last two participants to arrive, Andrew couldn't help reminiscing about his spy games as a boy back in Witte. These careful, clandestine adventures were much like his old escapades, but with much higher stakes. As a boy, he only risked punishment from Papa. Now, he risked exile, prison, and even death. With sudden surprise, Andrew realized he was right in the middle of the excitement he had longed for as a young man. God had given him his dreams of espionage after all!

When all the guests had arrived, they sat around a little table beneath a single light bulb hanging on a long cord. The windows were blocked with thick blankets, but even so, the tension in the room was so strong Andrew could almost taste it. They gathered at the table, heads bowed in prayer for the safety of the meeting they were about to hold. When the clock struck eight, Petroff stood.

"God has sent us a brother from Holland," he said, his voice barely above a whisper. "He will bless us tonight with a message from the Lord."

For twenty minutes, Andrew whispered words of encouragement to the little congregation. There were no hymns. Even quiet singing would have been far too risky. There was no offering. These people had already given their all for the cause of Christ. When Andrew finished sharing his heart with those faithful few, he nodded to Petroff.

With a grin, Petroff stood and carefully unwrapped the package. He then held up one of the Bulgarian Bibles that Andrew had brought. People gasped with joy, slapping their hands over their mouths to stifle the sound. They reverently passed the Bible from hand to hand, longing flowing through every fingertip. It had been years since many of them had seen a copy of God's Word, and now their tiny church would have its very own copy. Tears of joy mingled with embraces of thanks as they silently expressed their gratitude.

Andrew spent the rest of his visit to Bulgaria in a handful of unregistered underground churches. As he drank in the courage and consistency of worship in these services, Andrew was reminded of the command from Revelation 3:2 that God had given him in Poland: "Strengthen the things which remain." This tiny remnant of Bulgarian believers certainly needed strength, and Andrew spent his days and nights trying to minister to them in every way he knew how.

There were stories that broke his heart. There was a pastor who had gone to prison for eighteen months for baptizing teenagers. The night after his release, he baptized twenty-seven more eager teenagers in a muddy river outside of town. Another pastor had his church taken away and his license to preach revoked because he spoke to children about Jesus at a Christmas service. These stories were two among hundreds that reminded Andrew of the sacrifice and suffering of those behind the Iron Curtain. These stories gave him new resolve to carry out his calling.

Restrictions in Rumania

As he left Bulgaria and pulled up to the Rumanian border, Andrew felt the overwhelming rush of anticipation that had become familiar with each new nation he entered. There were only four cars ahead of him, and it seemed he might make it across within the hour. As he sat in his car and watched, however, he noticed the car at the front of the line was being torn apart. Every nook of the vehicle was being inspected while the helpless owner stood in the nearby grass.

"I wonder what they have against that poor fellow," Andrew thought to himself. "They're certainly being thorough with his car."

The next car was inspected just as thoroughly. Andrew felt a gnawing nervousness in the pit of his stomach. He thought of the Rumanian Bibles stowed in several secret compartments. They were hidden well enough to evade a cursory inspection, but not to avoid detection in such a thorough search. He was certain the precious Bibles would be confiscated, and he wasn't sure what they would do with him.

The inspection of the car in front of Andrew took over an hour. The border guards pulled off the hubcaps, pulled out the seats, and even took out pieces of the engine. Andrew wondered if he should turn back. Perhaps the timing was wrong, he reasoned. Maybe he was not supposed to enter Rumania on that day. His mind raced and his heart trembled.

Then God brought to mind the stories Andrew had heard in Bulgaria. To fail in his mission while serving faithfully was not really failure at all, but to fail in his mission because of fear was to fail utterly. He knew what he had to do. He would borrow the bravery of the Bulgarian saints and face the border with the belief that God was in control.

As peace spread throughout his soul, Andrew knew there was one more thing he needed to do. If God was going to work a miracle—which He would most certainly have to do at that border crossing—He may as well make it a big one.

"God," Andrew prayed, wrestling a half-dozen Rumanian Bibles from their hiding places, "I want this miracle to be so great I could never take credit for it. So I am going to put these Bibles on the seat beside me. Then it will be undeniable that the victory came from you."

Andrew piled the Bibles on the seat next to him just as the border guard waved him forward. With a pounding heart and a cottony mouth, he inched the car up to the inspection point. The guard took Andrew's papers and passport to examine them. Andrew pulled the door handle to get out of the vehicle, but found the guard was leaning against it, preventing him from getting out. In less than a minute, the guard finished his examination of the paperwork, handed it back to Andrew, and waved him through the checkpoint.

Andrew sat still, stunned and silent. He had only been sitting there for a matter of seconds. Again, the guard waved him through. Could he possibly be done? Andrew slowly drove forward, expecting shouting guards to block his path. No one came. In his rearview mirror, Andrew could see the car behind him moving up to the checkpoint. He drove a little faster. He glanced back again and saw the guards pulling a man from the car and opening the engine compartment. With that, Andrew pressed eagerly on the gas pedal and sped down the open road. What a miracle he had just experienced!

Giddy with God's goodness, Andrew hurried toward the first town on his route. The Rumanian government required all travelers to submit a detailed itinerary of the cities they would visit and the dates and times they would be there. Travelers were closely monitored, and Andrew soon discovered the Rumanian people were closely monitored as well. Police checkpoints were everywhere, in every city and town, along busy highways and on narrow street corners.

On a sunshiny Sunday morning in the city of Cluj, Andrew approached the clerk at his hotel desk.

"Can you please give me directions to the nearest church?" Andrew asked.

The clerk scowled and reluctantly directed Andrew to a large church across town. Andrew had learned that the government in Rumania forced all smaller churches to merge together, requiring all professing believers from all denominations to meet together in one large building. Then the government seized the property of all the smaller churches and claimed it for the State.

Because they were limited to only a single service each week, members of the congregation were eager to hear God's Word. The service had already been going for more than an hour when Andrew arrived just after 10:00 am. The church was packed, and Andrew was invited up to the platform to sit, since he was a visiting foreigner. For three hours he sat, pressed against the organ, listening to sermons and songs.

After the service, Andrew approached the denominational secretary, a rotund man who spoke both Rumanian and German.

"I was wondering if we might go somewhere where we can talk," Andrew said.

The secretary shook his head, left the building, and hurried down the street as fast as his short legs would take him. Thinking he was heading to a safer place to talk, Andrew followed at a distance. The secretary disappeared into a small house on a quiet lane. Andrew waited, carefully checked the street for anyone who might be watching, and then knocked on the door.

After a minute, the secretary opened the door. He glanced furtively up and down the street. Then he pulled Andrew inside and slammed the door shut.

"What are you doing here?" he hissed at Andrew.

Andrew was stunned at the odd greeting, but he mustered a smile. "I came to talk to you," he said. "To see if there is anything I can do for you."

"What do you mean?" the secretary asked. "What could you do for us?"

"Well, Bibles, for example," Andrew said. "I have some. Do you need any?"

For a moment, the secretary's harsh expression softened. But in a flash, the hardened glare was back.

"You brought Bibles into Rumania?" he barked. "You smuggled Bibles across the border?"

Andrew smiled. "Yes. Do you need some?"

The secretary looked away. "No!" he said gruffly. "We do not need your Bibles and we do not need your help. We need you to leave us alone. You must never come to my house again, and you must never go to the house of any Rumanian believer. Do you understand?"

Less than a week later, Andrew met with other church leaders. In this instance, however, Andrew was welcomed and directed to wait in an office with his briefcase of Bibles. Soon a frail old man hobbled into the room, wheezing with the simple effort of crossing to the desk. He was Gheorghe, president of a national denomination, and the young man with him was Ion, the denomination secretary. But after the introductions, the conversation stalled. Andrew spoke no Rumanian, and neither man spoke English, Dutch, or German. They sat together, staring at one another, until Andrew noticed a well-worn Bible on Gheorghe's desk. He had an idea.

Andrew pulled out his own Dutch Bible and flipped the pages to 1 Corinthians 16:20. He held out the Bible to Gheorghe and Ion. The name of the book and the verse numbers were distinguishable even in another language, and Gheorghe quickly grabbed the Rumanian Bible from his desk and flipped to the verse Andrew had indicated. The two Rumanian men leaned together over the Bible and read the verse.

"All the brethren greet you. Greet ye one another with an holy kiss."

They looked at each other and then grinned at Andrew. Gheorghe's fingers flew through the familiar pages until he reached Proverbs 25:25. He showed it to Andrew. Andrew found it in his Dutch Bible and read it.

"As cold waters to a thirsty soul, so is good news from a far country."

Andrew laughed out loud, and Gheorghe and Ion joined him. Andrew turned to Philemon, verses 4 and 5. Gheorghe and Ion found the verses and smiled as they read in Rumanian.

"I thank my God, making mention of thee always in my prayers, hearing of thy love and faith which thou hast toward the Lord Jesus, and toward the saints …"

Ion took the weathered Bible from Gheorghe and scanned the next few verses of Philemon. He pointed to verse 7, and as Andrew read it in Dutch, tears pricked his eyelids.

"For we have great joy and consolation in thy love, because … the saints are refreshed by thee, brother."

For more than half an hour, Andrew conversed with Gheorghe and Ion solely through God's Word. They traded passages back and forth, finding everything they needed to say within those hallowed pages. When their time together was done, they were fast friends. Although they had not spoken a single word to one another out loud, their hearts had spoken the language of love. They had spoken the language of God.

After finally finding a Rumanian interpreter, Andrew spent the next two weeks traveling throughout the Rumanian countryside. As in Bulgaria, Andrew heard stories from Rumanian believers that challenged his personal faith. Many had grown faint and turned away from their faith to follow the simpler path of the State. Others left Rumania for places where they could exercise their faith more freely. But there were a stalwart few who stayed, by necessity or by choice, and clung desperately to their beliefs, regardless of circumstances. These were the stories that inspired Andrew.

In Transylvania, Andrew met a chicken farmer and his family. They still owned land, although the State had taken some of it as punishment for church activities. The government had also given this farmer an impossible quota of eggs that must be produced each year. To meet the quota, the farmer had to take some of his meager earnings and buy eggs at the market. Each year the quota was raised, and each year the farmer struggled to meet the demands.

"Why not leave Rumania?" Andrew asked after he had toured the humble farm. "Is your farm that important to you?"

The farmer and his wife shook their heads adamantly.

"We will eventually lose the farm," the farmer admitted. "We stay because we love Rumania. We love what she once was and what we believe she can be again. We stay because it is the right thing to do. Besides, if the faithful ones all leave, who will be left here to pray?"

But not everyone was as determined. Down the road, miles off the main thoroughfare, Andrew met a persecuted pastor's wife whose faith was fading fast. She shared her story—so like the many others he had heard—and she looked at Andrew with haunted eyes.

"I used to believe people were praying for us," she said. "I used to believe God was with us. But now it is easier to believe we are forgotten. Some days I think even God has forgotten us."

Andrew tried to reassure her that she was not forgotten. He wished he could convince every wondering soul. But his visa was almost expired, and Corrie's baby was due soon. With a heavy heart and promises to return as soon as he could, Andrew left his new Rumanian friends and headed back toward Holland. He had no idea how long it would be before his path led that way again.

Bigger Blessings and
Broader Horizons

After more than two months away from home, Andrew pulled into the little yard in Witte in the darkest hours of a mid-May night. Oblivious to the fact that his family was sleeping, he climbed exuberantly up the rickety ladder to the little loft he shared with Corrie.

"Corrie, I'm home! I'm finally home," he shouted.

Without a phone or any way to communicate that he was coming, Andrew's arrival was a complete surprise. Corrie stumbled out of bed and hugged him. She made him coffee, and they talked until the sun was high in the sky, catching up on a thousand moments they had missed together.

"At least I made it home in time for the baby," Andrew observed.

"If you hadn't, I would have never forgiven you," Corrie teased happily.

Andrew and Corrie's son, Joppie, was born on June 4, 1959. With his endless squalling and the need to find space for baby things in their already tight quarters, Andrew began to see the need for a house of their own.

Late spring turned into a sweltering summer, and the donation clothes began to pile up again. Andrew and Corrie knew they needed a solution, and they knew that God would have to open doors miraculously to meet their needs. Every day for a week, they brought their situation to God in prayer.

In a miraculous turn of events, Andrew and Corrie soon found themselves the owners of a small house on the edge of town. In a single afternoon, Andrew had learned of the availability of the house, spoken with the owner, borrowed the needed money, and purchased the property. God's presence in the transaction was undeniable, and owning a house opened doors for new ministry opportunities. The little cottage was a bit dilapidated, with plenty of work to do, but it was theirs, and it was home.

Throughout 1959 and 1960, Andrew divided his time between working on the house, speaking around Holland, and traveling behind the Iron Curtain. He revisited every country that would allow him in, making multiple trips to several countries. He took a guided tour through Russia, not to do mission work, but just to familiarize himself with the country and the culture. The need was growing, the work was growing, and Andrew was growing overwhelmed by the enormity of it all.

Through his speaking engagements and travel, Andrew was becoming increasingly famous. His name was becoming known throughout Western Europe. He worried that the more his name was repeated, the more likely it would be that visa applications would be denied. After much prayer, he decided to start using the moniker "Brother Andrew" in all of his speaking engagements. This gave him a greater sense of anonymity and reduced the likelihood of problems due to name recognition.

The biggest challenge for Andrew was the amount of time he had to be on the road. The demand was so great that he was gone nearly nine months of every year, traveling to countries where Bibles and encouragement were in short supply. He missed many of the special moments of Joppie's first year because he was on the road. Tempting job offers with good salaries came in, but Andrew easily turned them down. His work was hard and inconvenient, but he knew he was doing exactly what he was meant to do.

God continued to bless Andrew and Corrie, and they added a second son, Mark Peter, to their family in 1960. In 1961, a third son, Paul Denis was born. Andrew felt the pull of Corrie and the boys on his time. Every time he got comfortable at home, however, a letter would come from Eastern Europe, tattered and often opened already. It would express a need that Andrew could not ignore. He would look at Corrie, she would smile at him knowingly, and they would pack the bags together for yet another trip.

Eastern Europe was a changing landscape, and Andrew was just one man. On his first trip to Bulgaria, a group of believers had begged him to stay and hold meetings with them, but traveling to Rumania had seemed more important. By the time Andrew made it back to Bulgaria, a whole year later, the meetings were no longer possible because persecution in that area was so pronounced. Andrew began to see the need to have a team of like-minded men and women. What mountains might they move together?

A formal organization was out of the question. It would be too easily hampered by foreign governments. But in sleepless nights and fervent daydreams, Andrew began to envision a dynamic group, always changing, moving throughout countries with ease, accomplishing things Andrew could never do alone. If one member or team was arrested, the less organized they were, the better it would be. When the plans were solidified in Andrew's mind, he shared them with Corrie.

"Praise God," Corrie responded with tears in her eyes. "It is selfish, I know, but sometimes I long for your boys to know you in person, instead of just the stories I tell them of you. Perhaps with help, we could see you a bit more often."

Andrew had not realized how much his boys were growing up without him. Corrie's response was the confirmation he needed. He began to pray that God would lead him to a partner for his ministry. Andrew wanted to start with one person who he would train based on everything he had learned in his travels. Then they could each train another partner, and the team would grow as God led them to more individuals who could catch their vision.

"How do I know who God wants me to choose as a partner?" Andrew wondered aloud to Corrie one night.

"Have you considered He might just tell you when the right one comes along? Have you prayed and asked God to give you a name?" she asked.

Andrew laughed. He knew Corrie was right. Her faith was so simple and trusting that it grounded him. Andrew and Corrie bowed their heads right then and prayed. Immediately, a name popped into Andrew's mind. He knew God had chosen the perfect partner.

Hans Gruber was Dutch, like Andrew, but they had met in the refugee camps in Austria. Hans was a huge man, clumsy and awkward, but kind-hearted and reliable. He spoke horrible German, bumped into everything, and seemed terribly wrong for the job, while at the same time practically perfect. In spite of his awkwardness, he could speak for an hour and hold hundreds of people spellbound. He lived life with purpose and passion. Andrew knew he was the man for the job.

That night, Andrew wrote to Hans, asking if he might consider accompanying Andrew on an upcoming trip to Russia. It would be the first time Andrew traveled unguided into that difficult country. Restrictions had recently been eased, so it seemed like a natural time to add a partner to the journey. Hans wrote back in emphatic agreement. In sixth grade, he had looked at a map of Russia and felt an indescribable

understanding that someday God would use him in
that land. Decades later, Hans had never forgotten that
leading, and Andrew's letter was an answer to prayer.

Hans traveled to Witte to train with Andrew before
their journey. The first thing Andrew needed to teach him
was how to drive. Because it was becoming legendary
and too recognizable, the little blue Volkswagen had
been replaced with a lumbering station wagon. Under
Andrew's careful guidance, Hans folded his six-foot-
seven-inch frame behind the wheel, eager to learn.

Six hours later, Andrew wondered if it wouldn't
be easier to just do all the driving himself. Hans
could not seem to grasp the coordination required to
simultaneously use the gearshift and the clutch. Finally,
he threw up his hands in frustration.

"I will never learn," he moaned.

Deep inside, Andrew agreed, but he encouraged
Hans to keep trying. After days of practice, Hans still
had not obtained a driver's license, but the day came
when they had to leave for Russia. Andrew decided
Hans could drive using his learner's permit, and they
could not delay the trip any longer.

Andrew and Hans packed Bibles and camping gear,
food and cooking supplies carefully into the station
wagon. The tires bulged at the weight, but they held.
With one last look at the little house in Witte, Andrew
and Hans started on their two thousand mile journey
into the very heart of Communism: Moscow, Russia.

The Reality of Russia

As they rolled through West Germany, then East Germany, and then Poland, Andrew grew more nervous while Hans grew more excited. The closer they drew to the border, the more Andrew noticed the bulging tires and sagging chassis. They were carrying so much, and most of it was illegal by Russian standards. He wondered what kind of opposition they might face at the border.

The Russian border had only been open for a very short time, and Andrew and Hans were in the first handful of independent tourists to cross into Communist Russia. With this in mind, they devised a strategy. Only one of them would speak. The other would always be praying—silently and secretly— that God would blind the eyes of the guards to the contraband they were bringing into the country.

When they reached the border, Andrew swallowed hard and glanced at Hans.

"Here we go," he said with a grin.

They exchanged pleasantries with the border guards and exchanged their money for Russian rubles. Then the guards asked to inspect the vehicle. Andrew made small talk while Hans prayed fervently. In the end, the guard only asked them to open a few suitcases. He was far more interested in inspecting the engine of the car they were driving. Andrew was more than happy to show him anything he wanted to see in the engine compartment. After all, nothing was hidden there.

When they had discussed the engine for a few minutes, the guard stamped their papers and handed them back.

"Welcome to Russia," he said, waving them through the barricades.

The Russian journey, however, was only beginning. There were 700 miles to cross between the border and Moscow. As the miles rolled past, Andrew told stories from his guided trip to Russia in 1960, the memories flooding back to him with the familiar Russian countryside.

"On my first free Sunday," he told Hans, "I went to the only Protestant church in all of Moscow. I expected to see a tiny congregation huddled in a big, empty building. Instead, I found a line of people outside, waiting to squeeze into the already packed building."

"The church was alive then?" Hans asked.

"Alive?" Andrew laughed. "It was bursting at the seams! There were nearly two thousand people in a building that was designed for a thousand at best. They led me to a special balcony for foreigners. And then they began to sing."

Andrew recounted for Hans how the singing was so deep and strong it shook the windows. Offerings were passed, hand to hand, over the congregation's heads until they reached the front of the church. And there were two sermons, one right after the other. Then Andrew shared the behavior that had surprised him most.

"During the sermons, I noticed people were sailing paper airplanes from the back of the church to the front," he told Hans. "People were sending them down from the balconies too. All the airplanes were being caught and passed forward to the front of the church."

"Did you ever discover the purpose?" Hans wondered.

"Yes. The man next to me must have sensed my confusion," Andrew said, smiling at the memory. "He told me they were prayer requests, and they were being sent forward to be collected by the pastors. And when the sermons were done, some of the requests were read and then all two thousand people launched into a prayer service like nothing I had ever heard before."

After seemingly endless hours of rolling hills and wide fields, Andrew and Hans reached the broad, bustling streets of Moscow. They found their government-assigned campsite and set up their tent. Then they began to unload some of the heavy Russian Bibles. Andrew had pulled two Bibles from their hiding places when Hans hissed quietly at him.

"We have an observer," Hans whispered. "Be careful."

Andrew casually hid the Bibles beneath a map and pulled out the coffee pot and the little camp stove. He glanced at a man, dressed in green army fatigues, loitering near their campsite and frequently looking their way. As soon as Andrew started making coffee, the man strolled away. Andrew and Hans exchanged worried looks. How could they distribute the Bibles if they couldn't even manage to unload them?

To calm their spirits, they took a Bible and headed for the midweek service at the church Andrew had visited before. When they got there, they found 1200 people in attendance. Hans was thrilled to watch first hand everything Andrew had described to him.

After the service, Andrew and Hans dawdled in the foyer, hoping to make some new contacts. Throughout the service Andrew had not seen Ivanhoff, his main contact in the church from the previous trip to Russia, and he was hesitant to approach anyone else. As he strolled around the edges of the room, Andrew prayed that God would guide him to the right contacts. He searched the face of each person he passed, waiting for direction. A few feet away, Andrew could see Hans doing the same thing.

Suddenly, Andrew's eyes were drawn to a thin man with even thinner hair, resting wearily against a wall. Andrew knew that was their man. He could almost hear God's voice above the din of the crowded room. To check his perception, Andrew locked eyes with Hans.

"I think we have our man," Hans murmured before Andrew had a chance to speak. He nodded his head toward the same man Andrew had been watching.

In blessed agreement, Andrew and Hans approached the man. Hans tried to speak to him in broken Russian, but the man simply became more and more confused. Finally, Andrew tried speaking German. The man's face instantly brightened. He was a second-generation German immigrant whose family lived in Siberia, he explained. They still spoke German in the home.

"If you are from Siberia, why are you here?" Andrew asked. "Isn't Siberia nearly two thousand miles away?"

The man nodded. "You are correct. But I have come here on behalf of my church. We have 150 members, but no Bibles."

Andrew and Hans smiled at each other. They could already see where the conversation was going. Andrew felt his pulse quicken with excitement, as it did every time God used him to answer a heartfelt need.

"One day, I had a dream," the man continued. "It sounds crazy, but in my dream, God told me to go to Moscow to get a Bible for my church. At first I refused, because it made no sense. Bibles are just as scarce in Moscow as they are in Siberia. But finally I decided I had to try. So here I am."

Hans pulled the Russian Bible from under his arm. "You were told to come two thousand miles west to receive a Bible," he said. "We were told to travel two thousand miles east to give a Bible. God has brought us together, in this room, by His Spirit."

Hans handed the Bible to the Siberian man. The man took it, looked at it, and began to cry. He threw his arms around Andrew and Hans and thanked them in Russian and German. Andrew whispered that there were more Bibles, and if he would meet them at the church at ten o'clock the next morning, they could give him several to take back to his church. The man agreed, and they went their separate ways.

The next morning, carrying four Russian Bibles in carry-on bags, Andrew and Hans walked to the church. Ten o'clock came and went, and there was no sign of the Siberian. By 10:30, Andrew was beginning to worry. He jumped when a voice whispered in his ear at 10:45.

"Hello, Brother Andrew."

Andrew whirled around. It was Ivanhoff! They hugged like long lost-friends. Then Ivanhoff grew serious.

"The friend you met last night cannot meet you," he said. "There are always secret police at our services. They saw you speaking with him. It is too dangerous for him to be here today. The police visited him and warned him about meeting with foreigners."

Andrew's shoulders slumped. He had been so excited about the possibility of getting Bibles to a place he might never go. He wondered why God had orchestrated the meeting and then made it impossible. As Andrew struggled with his thoughts, Ivanhoff spoke again.

"Do you have what you were going to give him?"

"Yes," Andrew answered.

"How many?" Ivanhoff asked.

"Four."

Ivanhoff thought a moment. "Give them to me," he said. "I will make sure they get to your Siberian friend."

Andrew hesitated. Could he trust Ivanhoff? Or was it a trap? He closed his eyes in momentary prayer. Peace flooded his heart. He looked at Hans, and Hans nodded. They pulled the newspaper-wrapped Bibles from their bags and placed them in Ivanhoff's waiting arms.

"There are more, you know," Andrew said suddenly.

Ivanhoff looked around the room as though the walls had ears. "Keep your voices low. How many do you have?"

"More than a hundred," Hans whispered.

Ivanhoff's knees buckled slightly and his whole body swayed. He led them silently down a long corridor and stopped when it turned a corner.

"Are you serious?" Ivanhoff whispered. "You are not joking? Not exaggerating?"

Andrew and Hans nodded their heads solemnly. Ivanhoff's face contorted with hope and grief. Emotions battling beneath the surface threatened to emerge. He put down the Bibles he was carrying and held out his hands. The fingertips were deformed and the nails had been pulled out. Tears filled his eyes.

"I love my Lord," he said, "but I cannot go back to prison. I cannot endure that again. I cannot help you with your load of Bibles."

153

Andrew placed an understanding hand on Ivanhoff's shoulder. "I do not blame you, brother," he said softly. "Perhaps you know someone who can help us?"

The question hung in the air as Ivanhoff thought for a moment. Then his face brightened.

"Markov!" he said with a smile. "Markov will help you. I will make the plans. Meet him in front of the GUM department store at one o'clock this afternoon. He will find you." He scooped up the Bibles Andrew and Hans had given him for the Siberian. "I will deliver these," he told them. "No one will bother me over only four Bibles. But you...you must be careful. God be with you, brothers."

He spun on his heel and hurried down the corridor. Andrew and Hans returned to the campsite. They spent an hour in prayer for their mission. They prayed for protection. They prayed God would direct them to Markov. And they prayed the prayer that Andrew had begun praying the very first time he smuggled Bibles: "Make seeing eyes blind."

At exactly one o'clock, they pulled up in front of the department store. As they parked, a man climbed out of a car up the street and strolled past, making careful eye contact with Andrew. A few minutes later he walked back and stopped at the driver's window.

"Brother Andrew?" he said.

"You must be Markov," Andrew said. "Good to meet you, brother."

Markov nodded. "We are about to do something rather risky," he told them. "We are going to exchange all of these Bibles on the outskirts of Red Square."

Andrew raised his eyebrows. It sounded like a crazy plan to him. Red Square was the center of Communism. The government offices were there. It was the headquarters of everyone who wanted to stop Andrew, the town square of the godless government.

"Follow me," Markov called as he headed for his car.

Andrew and Hans followed Markov's car to a narrow side street that bordered Red Square. There, beside a large wall and in front of a whole row of houses, Markov opened the rear door of his car.

"Pray," Andrew ordered Hans.

While Hans prayed aloud, Andrew pulled out as many Bibles as he could carry. He dumped them into bags and boxes and ferried them to Markov's car. They made trip after trip, out in the open, never knowing who might be watching. They trusted that God would make seeing eyes blind, and He did.

"Thank you, brothers," Markov said, his eyes moist and his lips trembling. "By next week these Bibles will be in churches across Russia."

Markov jumped into his car and drove off. Andrew climbed back into the station wagon and grinned at Hans.

"Can I stop praying now?" Hans asked.

"Ah, Hans," Andrew said, laughing. "You know better than that. You must never stop praying. We still have to go to the Ukraine. And who knows what God has in store for us there!"

Pocket-Bible Possibilities

The trip through the Ukraine began fairly uneventfully. Andrew and Hans worked through the country on their way home from Russia, stopping at several churches along the way to distribute the box of Ukrainian Bibles they had. At a little church, however, when there were only two Bibles left, Andrew saw something that would change the course of his ministry.

A man in the church brought his family's dearest treasure to show to Andrew. It was a pocket-sized Ukrainian Bible. Andrew could hardly believe what he was seeing. The print was tiny, but clear. The pages were as thin as the skin of an onion.

"Is it the whole Bible?" Andrew asked in disbelief.

"It is absolutely complete," the man told him.

Andrew held the little volume up next to a full-sized Ukrainian Bible. The pocket version was only about a fourth the size of a regular Bible. Andrew was full of questions.

"Where was this Bible printed? Who was the publisher? Where was it purchased?" he asked.

The man just shook his head. "I have no idea," he apologized. "It has been in my family for some time. I do not know how or where it was purchased."

Andrew studied the pocket Bible carefully. He was fascinated by the concept and inspired by what it might do for his ministry. If a tiny Bible could be printed in Ukrainian, the same could be done with Russian and other difficult languages. The hiding places in his car that could hold only a dozen bulky Bibles could hold nearly fifty of these pocket versions. And these diminutive Bibles would be easier to conceal, and pass from person to person. A dream began to grow in Andrew's heart as he turned the pocket Bible over and over in his hand.

"I can see that this Bible has value for you," the owner of the pocket Bible said. "So I have a proposal for you. Leave your remaining two full-sized Ukrainian Bibles with our church, and I will give you my pocket Bible."

Andrew was ecstatic. The trade was made, and they left the town with the precious pocket version of the Bible. Andrew planned to take it home to Holland. If he could find a publisher to undertake such a project, he could change the world with these compact—but complete—Bibles.

On their last Sunday in the Ukraine, Andrew and Hans visited a church near the Hungarian border. The pews were packed with nearly a thousand people. They prayed fervently. They sang in a thunderous chorus. But when the time came for the sermon, the pastor stepped down from the platform. One member handed the pastor a large book. As the pastor opened the book he had borrowed and began to read, Andrew realized it was a Bible. The pastor was expected to lead a thousand souls with no Bible of his own!

After the service, Andrew and Hans met with the pastor. The pastor quoted verses, and Andrew looked them up in his little Dutch Bible. The pastor watched him carefully. Finally, he looked wistfully out across the gray streets of the city.

"You know," he admitted, "I have no Bible of my own."

Andrew's heart was broken. They had already distributed every Ukrainian Bible they had brought. They had nothing to give the pastor. Except...there was the little pocket Bible, tucked underneath the driver's seat of the station wagon. Andrew hesitated. He had planned to use that as a template, a tool to convince a publisher to make thousands just like it. But the needs of the pastor and his congregation weighed heavily on Andrew. He jumped out of his seat.

"Wait here, brother," he told the pastor. "I have something for you."

He dashed to the car and pulled out the Bible. When he came back in and put in on the desk, the pastor just stared at it.

"What is it?" he finally asked.

"A Bible," Andrew answered. "It is your Bible now. You won't ever need to borrow one again."

The pastor reached for the Bible. With shaking hands, he picked it up and thumbed through it. Then, with a triumphant shout, he called the church elders into the room. There was a joyous exchange in Ukrainian, and then all the elders began embracing Andrew and Hans, weeping their thanks.

When they were back in the car, headed for the Hungarian border, Hans turned to Andrew.

"I thought you were saving that Bible to show to publishers," he said.

"I was," Andrew admitted. "But for me to carry two Bibles when someone has none..." His voice trailed off.

"I understand," Hans said.

"The thing is," Andrew continued, "I thought I knew why God gave us the pocket Bible. I thought it was for the publishers. But now I see God really gave us that Bible to give to that pastor. At times like these, I realize that I do not see God's big picture, and that my ways are not His ways." He paused and glanced at Hans. "I am still a student, still so small and helpless and foolish compared to the greatness of the God I serve."

Back in Holland, the idea of a pocket Bible became an obsession for Andrew. He talked to every publisher, every Bible society, every person he could think of. They all agreed there was merit in the idea, but no one had the cash needed to produce the new Bibles. Finally, Andrew started a fund for the Bibles. He felt the impatience of need settling into his heart, but he knew the money would come for the pocket Bibles in

God's time, and he had come to understand that God's time was always the right time.

In the meantime, there was more work to be done than Andrew and Hans could keep up with. Even when they split up to tackle two countries at once, requests for Bibles and pleas for help and encouragement poured in. It was beginning to feel like for every need they met, two or three needs went unaddressed. They were wearing down, wearing out, and wearing thin.

"We need to add another member to our team," Hans insisted one sticky summer night in 1962. They immediately plunged into a time of prayer.

"What about Rolf?" they said at exactly the same moment, raising their heads.

Andrew laughed. "Well, I guess that settles it. Rolf will be our new team member."

That night, Andrew wrote to Rolf, a Dutch student just finishing his graduate seminary work. At first Rolf was resistant, but within days, he was convinced of God's leading. Uncertain of his abilities, but certain of his calling, Rolf joined the team and immediately left with Hans on a trip to Rumania. When Rolf returned, any remaining doubts had been swept gloriously away. He had caught the vision, and he could not wait for his next trip.

In spite of all the progress, the pocket Bibles remained a pipe dream. The best bid they could find for 5000 Bibles was $15,000, and after a year of donations, they had only managed to save $2000. In desperation, Andrew looked across the table at Corrie one night.

"How much do you think we could sell our house for, Corrie?" he asked.

Corrie's face was the color of milk. She rubbed her swollen belly and stared at Andrew with wide eyes. "Andy, we have a baby coming and three little boys already. We cannot sell the house."

A few weeks later, baby Stephanie arrived. The next few months were absorbed by the bustle of a new baby. One night, after the children were in bed, Corrie came to Andrew again.

"Andy, I don't need the house anymore," she said decidedly. "I don't know where we will live or what we will do, but I am willing."

Andrew studied her eager face. "Are you sure?"

She nodded, her eyes shining. "Remember what we used to say?" she reminded him. "We don't know where the road will lead …"

"But we will walk the road together," Andrew finished. He hugged her. "I remember."

Although they put the house on the market, no one came to look at it. One afternoon, Andrew received a call from the Dutch Bible Society. They told Andrew they could not get his pocket-Bible dream out of their minds and off their hearts. If he could arrange for printing, they offered to pay half the cost of each Bible. In addition, they would pay for the printing upfront, and Andrew could buy the Bibles from them as needed.

Andrew could hardly breathe. This arrangement made the Bibles so affordable they would not have to sell the house after all. When he told Corrie, they did a dance of joy around the kitchen. God acknowledged their willingness to surrender everything by giving them more than they could have ever expected. The pocket Bibles were going to be a reality! In 1964, the first batch of pocket Bibles arrived in Witte, and the entire household burst into rejoicing.

On the 16th of May, while flowers blossomed and the polders came to life, Andrew and Rolf headed for Russia with 650 pocket Bibles. They had heard a Bible was now worth as much as a cow in Russia, the equivalent of hundreds of dollars. According to Russian law, anyone caught smuggling something so valuable would be put to death by a firing squad. They understood the risk was great, but they knew the need was greater.

The first Sunday in Moscow they went to the grand church, the same one where Andrew had taken Hans. It was as packed as ever, and Andrew immediately spotted Ivanhoff on the platform. Ivanhoff glanced up and his eyes met Andrew's. A tiny smile played across his lips, and he slipped from the platform.

After the service, Andrew and Rolf scanned the crowd in the foyer, hoping to see Ivanhoff's familiar face. A loud voice near Andrew's ear made him jump.

"Welcome to Russia," the voice boomed.

Andrew spun around. It was Markov. They grinned at each other. Andrew introduced Rolf.

"Welcome to Russia, Rolf," Markov said, speaking loudly to avoid suspicion.

"We brought gifts," Andrew said, trying to equal Markov's volume.

"Wonderful!" Markov exclaimed, drawing the word out.

"Can we go somewhere to talk?" Andrew wondered.

Markov suggested their previous meeting spot, just off Red Square. Andrew shuddered. He was not fond of taking such risk.

"I would like to try something different," he said.

Markov lowered his voice. He told them to meet him at five o'clock under the big blue "Moscow" sign on the road to the city of Smolensk. Andrew and Rolf agreed, and they all drifted apart, as casually as possible.

As Rolf drove their new van around Moscow that sunny afternoon, Andrew climbed into the back and unpacked the Bibles. They would need to move fast when making the transfer, Andrew knew, and the pocket Bibles would need to be out of their hiding places and ready to go. As the time of their rendezvous neared, Andrew and Rolf were shaking with anticipation and fear. Suddenly, Rolf looked at Andrew.

"Why are we so frightened?" he asked. "We are doing the work of the Lord, and He is in control. He cares for the sparrows, so why do we assume he does not care for us?"

With that declaration, Rolf began to lustily sing a hymn. Soon, Andrew joined in, and the van vibrated with song as it rolled down the road to Smolensk. At exactly five o'clock, they pulled off the road under the big blue sign. A few moments later, Markov passed in his van, flashing his lights at them. They pulled out and followed him to a busy shopping center where dozens of people were loading and unloading packages. In broad view of scores of shoppers, Andrew and Rolf spent five minutes transferring boxes of Bibles to Markov. With a quick goodbye, the Bibles were on their way to fill needs in every corner of the vast Russian landscape.

"Once again, Lord," Andrew prayed thankfully, "you have made seeing eyes blind. I thank you for these hundreds of Bibles that will proclaim your Word far and wide. But I still feel there is something more I should do. Somewhere else I should go. Show me, Lord. Here am I, send me."

The Chinese Challenge

Andrew's answer came from God through an unusual encounter on a Moscow bus later that year. There were many Chinese refugees living in Russia in 1964, so Andrew didn't think it was odd that he ended up sitting on the bus next to a well-dressed Chinese man. The one thing that did stand out was the tiny gold cross that was pinned to the man's lapel. Andrew asked him about it.

"I am the secretary of the YMCA in Shanghai, China," the man said in perfect English.

"There is still a YMCA functioning within China?" Andrew asked in disbelief.

"Of course," the man said proudly. "You must visit me and see for yourself."

He handed Andrew a business card. Andrew slipped the card into his pocket and chatted with the man until his stop. When the Chinese man left, Andrew pulled the business card back out. He knew God had something new in store for him, but the thought of going to China intimidated him. Andrew had never considered going somewhere so far away, somewhere he couldn't possibly blend into a crowd.

As the months passed, Andrew couldn't shake the feeling that God had a plan for him in China. When an opportunity came to speak in California in 1965, Andrew decided to travel to Taiwan afterwards and then on to Hong Kong and China.

When he arrived in Hong Kong, he discovered his enthusiasm may have eclipsed solid research and careful planning. Missionaries there laughed at his certainty that he would get a visa to China.

"They don't give visas to anyone these days," one told him. "Not to people who have recently visited America."

Andrew closed his ears to these warnings. Instead, he walked confidently into the Chinese Travel Office, the government entity responsible for granting visas. He waited in a long line, praying the whole time.

"Next," the clerk called.

Andrew stepped up. "Good morning, sir."

The Chinese clerk frowned at him. "Have you recently been to either Taiwan or the United States?" he asked.

"As a matter of fact," Andrew admitted, "I have just come from Taiwan. And before that, I was in California."

The clerk handed Andrew's passport back to him without even looking in it. "There is no point in applying then," he insisted. "These are the enemies of China. You will be denied entry."

"Please," Andrew said, "just give me the paperwork. I will fill it out. And if you are correct and I am denied a visa, so be it."

Shaking his head, the clerk angrily pushed a stack of papers at Andrew. "Next," he called loudly.

Andrew took the papers and eagerly filled them out. He returned them to another clerk, who promised a response in three days. For those three days, Andrew prayed God would miraculously grant the visa. He prayed he would know what to say once he was inside China. He prayed God would move mountains and move hearts so His purposes could be accomplished.

On the morning of the third day, Andrew received a message at his hotel. It was from the Chinese Travel Office asking him to call them back. Instead, Andrew traipsed down to the office, a goofy grin plastered on his face. He had a feeling God was about to do something wonderful, a feeling that was confirmed when he walked back out the door less than an hour later with his Chinese visa and travel documents.

The next morning, Andrew boarded a train bound for Communist China. He wasn't sure what to expect or what he would find, but he was sure that God would be with him. He left most of his clothing behind in the hotel in Hong Kong, and he filled his suitcase with Chinese Bibles and booklets he had purchased at a little Bible shop near the hotel. He was determined not to enter China empty-handed.

At a little town on the Chinese border, the train stopped. Those continuing into Communist China would have to cross the border on foot, as trains did not make the journey. When his group was ready and the guide had arrived, they crossed the bridge in two short lines. In the middle of the bridge, Andrew noticed a slight change in paint color on the steel girders, and he knew he had just taken his first step into China.

At the other side of the bridge, they walked to a checkpoint bordering a large factory complex. Everything seemed grayer than in Hong Kong. The buildings were gray, the streets were gray, the uniforms were gray. The only splash of color was found in the carefully planted rows of crimson geraniums that bordered the walkway to the checkpoint.

Inside the little checkpoint building, a smiling girl motioned Andrew to her station. He walked over, lugging his little suitcase. The lack of space inside had prevented any concealment of the Bibles and booklets he had brought. If he were asked to open the suitcase, his plans would be obvious.

"Please open your suitcase, sir," the girl said in English, with a wide smile.

Andrew swallowed hard and carefully unzipped his case. He flung the lid open and watched the girl's puzzled expression. She studied the contents of his suitcase and then looked up at Andrew.

"Do you have a watch, sir?" she asked. "And are you carrying a camera?"

Andrew shook his head. The girl zipped the suitcase closed and pushed it toward him.

"Welcome to China, sir," she said, motioning for the next person in his group.

As Andrew walked away, realization flooded his mind. The girl had not questioned him about the Bibles because she had not known what they were. It was suddenly clear to him that this bright-faced girl in her twenties had never seen a Bible in her life.

Andrew made his way through China, trying to absorb as much of the culture as possible. The cities seemed clean and the people educated, in contrast to what he had seen in Eastern Europe. There was a godlessness, however, that he recognized. People had no interest in seeking God to fulfill their needs; their god was the government.

When he finally reached Shanghai, Andrew went straight to the YMCA offices and asked for the secretary he had met in Moscow. The clerk at the front desk looked at him blankly.

"I'm sorry, sir," she said. "We have no one by that name here."

"But you must," Andrew insisted. "I met him."

The clerk went into a back room and came back a few moments later. "No, sir," she apologized. "No one recognizes that name. That person does not work here."

"He was your secretary for many years," Andrew said adamantly, pulling out the business card. "Someone must know who he is and where he is."

The clerk disappeared again. She was gone for a long time. When she came back, the pleasant smile was gone from her face. Her tone was clipped, and she refused to look Andrew in the eye.

"I'm sorry, sir," she said. "He is out of town, and no one knows when he will return."

Andrew later learned it was common for believers in China to go "out of town" and never return. The people were so enthralled by their government, however, they were willing to close their eyes to their disappearing brothers. Andrew found this attitude of practiced apathy difficult to break through, especially with regards to witnessing.

Throughout China, Andrew tried to hand out Bibles, but no one would take them. They weren't afraid. No, these people were just completely disinterested in the message. In desperation, Andrew took to leaving Bibles and booklets in hotels, but the desk clerks would always track him down to return his items.

When Andrew found himself in Peking on a Sunday morning, he asked his tour guide to take him to church.

"There are very few churches here," the guide said. "Especially Protestant churches. But I will see if I can find one."

After an hour, the guide found a church. Andrew entered the drab sanctuary just as the service was starting. The little congregation was aged and joyless, stumbling through an out-of-tune hymn. An ancient pastor with a stringy gray beard gave a short sermon, and most of the people in the pews were sleeping before he was finished. Andrew had seen this attitude all across China. The government held the hearts of the young people, and they knew religion would die with the older generations.

"In the communes, sir, you will find no churches," the leader of a Communist commune of 10,000 people proudly told Andrew. "You see, religion is for the helpless. Here in China we are not helpless anymore."

As Andrew left China and headed home to Holland, his burden for the Chinese people was deeper than ever, but he recognized ministry in China would take a different strategy than ministry in Eastern Europe. He knew God would give him a strategy when the time was right. Until then, other nations were crying out, and Andrew was ready to answer the cry.

The Morphing Ministry

By the mid 1960s, the landscape of Communism was beginning to change, but the work was far from done. There were new countries to explore and old countries to revisit. There were Bibles to smuggle, believers to encourage, and borders to breach. There was more work than Andrew, Hans, and Rolf could undertake. In 1965, they added Marcus to their team.

That same year, Andrew and Hans took a trip to Cuba, the only Communist nation in the West. They found sun-drenched seaside villages and the hustle and bustle of Havana. They found easy acceptance from the people and undeniable opposition from the police. In the interest of time and the enormity of the task, Andrew and Hans split up, with Andrew staying in and around Havana while Hans went east to the Oriente province. By the time they left a few weeks later, Andrew and Hans felt God had given great progress in Cuba.

Later in 1965, Rolf and Marcus went to Albania, the last "closed" Communist country. They traveled as teachers with a French tour group. Although there was no official Albanian language—only three difficult dialects—Rolf and Marcus were able to take in booklets and Bible literature, even though the law strictly prohibited it. They found, however, that no one wanted their literature. The people were kind, but vague, and Rolf and Marcus felt all they ever saw was a façade of what Albania really was. They left Albania with a sense of frustration and fervent prayers for the future.

The future was opening up for Andrew and his team. By 1967 it had grown to nearly a dozen members. The goal was to visit every Eastern European country at least once each year. Some countries could be visited multiple times each year. Andrew and his team made return trips to Cuba and initial trips into North Korea and Vietnam. God's Word was overcoming obstacles and opposition in nations around the globe, all because of the willing workers on Andrew's team.

As politics changed, Andrew's ministry changed by necessity. Yugoslavia began allowing Bibles into the country freely at about the same time Hungary cracked down on Christian activities. Bibles were burned in China as beliefs were ignited in other Communist nations. To keep up, Andrew and his team had to be flexible, constantly open to new needs and new ways of meeting those needs.

With the influx of visitors from the West in the 1970s and 1980s, the noose of Communism began to loosen. In many countries, tourists were welcomed, and most nations stopped prosecuting visitors for bringing in a Bible or two for their personal use. This new thinking birthed a dream in Andrew's heart.

"I just thought of something," he said to Hans one day. "Let's say of the thousands of tourists who flood Eastern Europe each year, maybe a thousand of them are believers."

"The number is probably more than that," Hans responded.

"Well, I know, but for argument's sake, let's say only a thousand of them are believers," Andrew said. "Do you understand what that means?"

Hans tipped his head and thought a moment. Then he slowly shook his head. He wasn't sure where Andrew's mounting passion was leading.

"Hans, what if every one of those thousand believers brought just one Bible into the country with them," Andrew said. "And what if they just happened to leave that Bible behind. Do you realize how many Bibles we could get into Eastern Europe in just one year? Far more than we can carry in our cars!"

Hans caught Andrew's excitement. It became a theme when they spoke in churches throughout Western Europe and America. They encouraged tourists to become incidental missionaries by simply leaving a Bible behind. Thousands of tourists responded to the call, and abandoned Bibles began popping up across Eastern Europe.

Out of these mini-missions endeavors, Andrew founded Open Doors. It was a formal organization, which he had originally tried to avoid, but it served the purpose of uniting those whose hearts were burdened for getting the gospel light to those in the darkness of Communism. But the missionary tourism that Open Doors advocated and used throughout Eastern Europe was not possible in China, and the godlessness of the Chinese people still weighed heavily on Andrew's heart.

An answer for China finally came, although not until 1981. Early in the year, Open Doors purchased a barge and a tugboat. At the same time, in Nashville, Tennessee, Bible publishing company Thomas Nelson was printing one million Chinese New Testaments. All the pieces were in place for a massive mission, and each step was taken in earnest prayer. They only had one attempt, only one chance to get things right. Everything had to be perfect.

On June 18th, 1981, Project Pearl was launched. At high tide in Swatow, China, under the cover of a moonless night, 232 one-ton water tight packages of Bibles were floated from the barge to the beach. Word of the operation was secretly spread through a network of underground churches, and thousands of Chinese believers flocked to the little fishing village. As the packages floated up and lodged themselves on the sandy beach, people poured from the dunes to tear open the packages and whisk the Bibles to safety. By the time the Chinese Army made it to the isolated beach in Swatow more than two hours later, most of the Bibles were gone, well on their way to the hands of house churches all across China.

As small steps were made in China, the face of Eastern Europe was changing dramatically. By the late 1980s, Communism was beginning to crumble. By the turn of the millennium, Eastern European Communism was found primarily in history books, although Communist regimes in Cuba, China, and North Korea were still going strong. Just because the Iron Curtain had been drawn, however, Andrew did not feel his work was done. In between speaking engagements and trips to encourage pastors, Andrew spent a great deal of time in prayer. How would God use him next? He was sure there were still big things ahead.

Walking Through Open Doors

Nearly six decades since Andrew stepped off the train into the sticky summer air of Communist Poland, his ministry continues. Open Doors has expanded to become a multinational group with hundreds of workers in dozens of countries. The work of one man has become the work of many, changing the world for Christ. Andrew's vision of individuals and teams putting God's Word in hands around the globe has truly become a reality.

As for Andrew himself, he lives much as he did when his ministry began. He avoids technology as much as possible and tries to keep his focus on the still, small voice of God. Each year God gives him new direction and new passions. He frequently reminds those involved with Open Doors that as believers we are not to be anti-anything, we are to be pro-Jesus. That is how we make a difference.

When Communist Russia collapsed, Open Doors orchestrated the importation of a million New Testaments. Andrew carried the one millionth Bible into Russia himself, celebrating a long-held dream of Bibles being readily available throughout Eastern Europe. He has continued reaching out to existing Communist countries like China, North Korea, Cuba, and others. He believes God's Word is for everyone, and he feels his work is far from done.

In addition to carrying Bibles—both openly and in secret—Open Doors supports families of those who are killed for the sake of the gospel. They offer scholarships to seminary students from nations where the gospel still cannot be openly preached. They give cars to missionaries so they can expand their ministries. They also provide small printing presses, so missionaries can print Bibles and booklets for themselves.

Today, Andrew's main ministry is to the Islamic world, focusing on countries in the Middle East and North Africa. He travels to these nations frequently, trying to reach new converts and striving to encourage believers who face persecution. Even though he is not always allowed to speak in Islamic nations, Andrew recognizes the fact that his mere presence can be a blessing to believers.

Throughout the Islamic world, Andrew is pioneering the concept of "being there evangelism." He believes our greatest opportunities to witness often come from us just being present in the world of those who need Christ. He stresses the need for Christian plumbers, doctors, teachers, police officers, and workers in every profession. He encourages believers to establish their businesses in Islamic nations and neighborhoods.

"Wherever believers are," Andrew reminds his listeners, "Jesus is there too!"

When people express their fear at being caught sharing their faith, and their terror at being imprisoned or killed for Christ, Andrew shares his story. He understands the fear, because he has walked through it. He understands the uncertainty, because he has conquered it. He understands the terror, because he has faced it head-on.

"The outside world is not a threat to us," Andrew proclaims knowingly. "It is a challenge, but never a threat."

Andrew believes in a big God, a God who made seeing eyes blind. A God who made the impossible possible. A God who opened locked doors. And knowing this God intimately, Andrew is spurred onward by the words of Jesus in Matthew 28:18-20:

"All power is given unto me in heaven and in earth. Go ye therefore, and teach all nations, baptizing them in the name of the Father, and of the Son, and of the Holy Ghost: teaching them to observe all things whatsoever I have commanded you: and lo, I am with you always, even unto the end of the world."

This command is always present in Andrew's mind, always prompting his passionate steps. He believes God opened a door with this command, a door that has never been closed. And as long as there are open doors, Andrew will walk through them, emboldened by the belief that God will be with him.

Brother Andrew Timeline

1928   Andrew van der Bijl is born on May 11.

1939   Andrew's brother Bas dies of tuberculosis. World War II officially begins with the German invasion of Poland.

1940   Germany invades Holland and begins the occupation of Witte.

1941   The United States enters World War II after the attack on Pearl Harbor, Hawaii.

1945   World War II officially ends with the surrender of Germany and Japan.

1946   Andrew joins the Dutch Army.

1948   Mama dies while Andrew is in Indonesia.

1949   Andrew is shot while in the army. Returns to Holland. While in rehabilitation, he attends a revival service where God speaks to him.

1950   Andrew asks God to forgive his sins. He gets a job at Ringers' Factory, meets Corrie van Dam, and surrenders his life to be a missionary.

1953   Andrew goes to WEC in London to train as a missionary.

1955   Andrew graduates from WEC and travels to Poland, Czechoslovakia, Yugoslavia, and Hungary, smuggling Bibles. He also works in refugee camps in West Germany and Austria.

1958   Andrew and Corrie are married in Alkmaar, Holland. Andrew and Corrie work together in the refugee camps and in Yugoslavia.

1959   Andrew visits Bulgaria and Rumania. Joppie, Andrew's first son, is born in Witte.

1959	Andrew travels throughout Europe, distributing tracts and encouraging pastors.
1960	Mark Peter, Andrew's second son, is born.
	Andrew becomes one of the first to take a guided tour of Communist Russia.
1961	Paul Denis, Andrew's third son, is born.
	Andrew travels to Russia and the Ukraine. He sees his first pocket Bible.
	The Berlin Wall is erected.
1963	Stephanie, Andrew's daughter, is born.
1964	The first Russian pocket Bibles are completed, 650 of them are carried into Russia.
1965	Andrew travels to China. Andrew travels to Cuba.
1967	The ministry team grows. Every Communist European country is visited once per year.
	The book *God's Smuggler* is released.
1967+	Open Doors, Brother Andrew's ministry group, expands to reach millions living under the influence of Communism and other oppressive forces.
1981	Project Pearl takes place, delivering a million Bibles to the Chinese people waiting on the beaches of Swatow.
1989	Andrew hand delivers the one millionth Bible to Russia.
1992	Project Samuel; Chinese Study Bible.
1997	Andrew receives Religious Liberty Award from World Evangelical Fellowship.
2008	Open Doors ministers to Chinese Christians during the Olympics.
2012	Open Doors Volunteer Summit.

For more information about Brother Andrew and Open Doors visit the following website:

www.opendoors.org

Thinking Further Topics

Chapter 1:
Matthew 7:20 says, " … by their fruits ye shall know them." What does it mean to be known by your "fruits"? What did the "fruit" of Andrew's early life say about him? What do your "fruits" say about you?

Chapter 2:
From 1939 through 1940, Andrew experienced a number of sad and scary things. Read Isaiah 43:1-2. What do these verses tell us about God's love for us and His presence with His children? How was God with Andrew during these times? How has God been with you during tough situations?

Chapter 3:
Have you ever made a bad choice and then felt unworthy of forgiveness? While in the Army, Andrew made some bad choices. He felt like he could never be forgiven. 1 John 1:9 says, "If we confess our sins, he is faithful and just to forgive us our sins, and to cleanse us from all unrighteousness." Are any sins too big for God to forgive? Why or why not?

Chapter 4:
In the rehabilitation facility, Andrew began to read his Bible. God's Word gave him hope. Read Psalm 119:105. How does the Bible help us understand God? How does it give you hope and light in your life?

Chapter 5:
Matthew 5:16 says, "Let your light so shine before men, that they may see your good works, and glorify your Father which is in heaven." When Andrew first took the job at Ringers' Chocolate Factory, he was surrounded by a lot of spiritual darkness. He chose to make the factory his mission field. How can you be a light for Jesus in your neighborhood? Your school? Your family?

Chapter 6:
The philosophy of WEC was to send missionaries out with virtually no financial support. Kees told Andrew this was biblical, based on Matthew 10. Can you find the verses Kees was referring

to? Do you agree or disagree with the practice and philosophy of WEC? Why?

Chapter 7:

While at WEC, Andrew learned to trust God for all his needs. Read Philippians 4:19. What does Paul say about our needs in this verse? How did God provide for Andrew's needs while he was at WEC? How has God provided for your needs?

Chapter 8:

Near the end of Andrew's trip to Poland God gave Andrew the words of Revelation 3:2 to motivate his ministry. Read this verse. What do you think it means to "strengthen what remains?" How did those words apply to Andrew's ministry? How can you apply them to your life?

Chapter 9:

In his prayer at the Yugoslavian border, Andrew asked God to make seeing eyes blind. What does that mean? Does God still do miracles? Have you ever experienced a miracle—big or small—in your life? What did God do for you?

Chapter 10:

Matthew 16:24 says, " … if any man will come after me, let him deny himself, and take up his cross, and follow me." What does Jesus mean when he tells us to take up our cross? How do we see this reflected in the lives of Andrew, Professor B, Janos, and others? What can you do to be a better follower of Jesus?

Chapter 11:

Andrew and Corrie were missionaries wherever God placed them. Wherever they went, they looked for opportunities to share Jesus with others. Can you be a missionary and minister to those around you? How can you share Jesus with the people God has placed in your life?

Chapter 12:

Read Proverbs 3:5-6. What does it mean to have God direct your paths? When Andrew had to make a massive detour to get to Bulgaria and Rumania, he was discouraged. But God had things to teach him. Does God direct your path? How can you trust Him more and give Him more control over your life?

Chapter 13:

The believers in Bulgaria were faithful despite persecution. In 2 Timothy 4:7, Paul wrote, "I have fought a good fight, I have finished my course, I have kept the faith." How did the Bulgarian believers live out this verse? How can you fight the "good fight" and keep strong faith in your life?

Chapter 14:

When Andrew met with Ion and Gheorghe in Rumania, they spoke "the language of God." What does that mean? How did they communicate with each other? Compare and contrast Andrew's meeting with Ion and Gheorghe with his meeting with the denominational secretary the week before. Do you see both of these attitudes at work in the world around you?

Chapter 15:

Read 1 Corinthians 4:2. What does it mean to be a faithful steward? How can you be a faithful steward in your life?

Chapter 16:

The exchange of Russian Bibles took place right beside Red Square, the very heart of Communism, in full view of several homes and businesses. Do you believe this was too great a risk? Does God want us to take risks or to choose safer paths?

Chapter 17:

In the Ukraine, Andrew believed he knew why God gave him the pocket Bible, but God showed Andrew a different plan. Read Isaiah 55:8-9. How did Andrew open his heart to God's plans? Has God ever had a different plan for you than you had for yourself? Was it easy or difficult to change your plans so they matched up with God's plan? Why?

Chapter 18:

Isaiah 55:11 says, "So shall my word be that goeth forth out of my mouth: it shall not return unto me void." This verse promises that wherever God's Word is spoken, it will have an impact. How does this verse relate to Andrew's trip to China? Was his trip pointless, since no one seemed to listen? How can you use this verse in your life?

Chapter 19:

As the world changed, Open Doors changed too, adapting to accomplish great things for God. Mark 10:27 reminds us, "With God all things are possible." What seemingly impossible things did Open Doors accomplish? What "impossible" things do you want God to do in your life?

Chapter 20:

Andrew's ministry is still driven by Matthew 28:18-20. What directions did Jesus give His followers in these verses? How does Open Doors follow these commands? How can you live out these verses today?

Author's Notes

I first heard about Brother Andrew when I was eight years old. I was fascinated by his drive and daring. I was intrigued by his adventures. I was also inspired by his faithfulness. He did not live a life free from fear, but he was faithful through his fear, allowing God to triumph over seemingly impossible circumstances.

As I researched this book, I was impacted deeply by Brother Andrew's influence. I read biographies about him, researched Open Doors, and watched videos of Brother Andrew speaking to groups over the past few decades. With every new bit of information, one impression stayed strong in my mind: passion. Andrew has a deep passion for sharing Jesus with the world.

Brother Andrew's passion should do three things for us. First, it should inspire us to share God honestly and fearlessly with family, friends, and neighbors. Second, it should encourage us to look for new ways to work for God, whether easy or difficult. Third, it should prompt us to learn more about God and His Word.

Brother Andrew's journey is simply the result of one man who chose to follow God step-by-step and day-by-day. In Matthew 28:20, God promises to be with us—just like He was with Brother Andrew—if we choose to faithfully walk with Him: "Lo, I am with you always, even unto the end of the world."

Nancy Drummond

Bibliography

Biographical Sources

"Andrew van der Bijl." Wikipedia.
http://en.wikipedia.org/wiki/Brother_Andrew.

Benge, Geoff and Janet. *Brother Andrew: God's Secret Agent (Christian Heroes: Then & Now)*. Seattle: YWAM Publishing. 2006.

"Brother Andrew." Hyper History. www.hyperhistory. net/apwh/bios/b2brotherandrew.htm.

"Brother Andrew #1." Open Doors USA. You Tube. http://www.youtube.com/watch?v=NBAF8RNAb KQ&app=desktop.

"Brother Andrew Biography." Inspirational Christians. www.inspirationalchristians.org/brother-andrew/.

Brother Andrew and Elizabeth and John Sherrill. *God's Smuggler—35th Anniversary Edition*. Bloomington, MN: Chosen Books. 2001 ed.

"Brother Andrew of Open Doors—How Much Do We Really Care?" Kerugma Productions. You Tube. http://www.youtube.com/watch?v=nIqpuA2OMKc.

"Brother Andrew: Open Doors Volunteer Summit 2012." Open Doors UK & Ireland. You Tube. http://www.youtube.com/watch?v=uPYILNshQqw.

"Brother Andrew's Story." Open Doors USA.
www.opendoorsusa.org/about-us/brother-andrew/.

"History of Open Doors." Open Doors USA. www.
opendoorsusa.org/about-us/history-of-open-doors.

Meloche, Renee Taft and Bryan Pollard. *Brother Andrew: Taking Bibles to the World (Heroes for Young Readers)*. Seattle: YWAM Publishing. 2009.

"One With Them—Brother Andrew." Open Doors USA. You Tube. http://www.youtube.com/watch?v=259lzOS3KrA.

"The Beginnings of Open Doors with Brother Andrew." Open Doors UK & Ireland. You Tube. http://www.youtube.com/watch?v=srncqLLlZ2I.

Other Sources

"Communist Border Crossings." Yahoo Images Search. http://images.search.yahoo.com/search/images;_ylt =A0SO8ypzR5VS9CIAOYdXNyoA?p=Communist+ Border+Crossings&fr=yfp-t-900&fr2=piv-web.

"St. Pancras, Noord-Holland, Netherlands." Collins Maps. www.collinsmaps.com/maps/Netherlands/ Noord-Holland/St-Pancras/P391776.00.aspx.

CHRISTIAN FOCUS PUBLICATIONS

Christian Focus | Christian Heritage | CF4K | Mentor

Christian Focus Publications publishes books for adults and children under its four main imprints: Christian Focus, CF4K, Mentor and Christian Heritage. Our books reflect our conviction that God's Word is reliable and Jesus is the way to know him, and live for ever with him.

Our children's publication list includes a Sunday School curriculum that covers pre-school to early teens, and puzzle and activity books. We also publish personal and family devotional titles, biographies and inspirational stories that children will love.

If you are looking for quality Bible teaching for children then we have an excellent range of Bible stories and age-specific theological books.

From pre-school board books to teenage apologetics, we have it covered!

Find us at our web page:
www.christianfocus.com

CF4·K
Because you're never
too young to know Jesus